RAYMOND MOl

PROBLEMS IN THEOLOGY

❈ *The Knowledge of Christ*

CONTINUUM
London & New york

**Continuum**
Wellington House, 125 Strand, London WC2R 0BB
370 Lexington Avenue, New York, NY 10017-6550

First published 1999

British Library Cataloguing-in-Publication Data
A catalogue record for this book is available from the British Library.

ISBN 0–8264–5130–6

Typeset by York House Typographic
Printed and bound in Great Britain by Redwood Books, Trowbridge

O the mind, mind, has mountains; cliffs of fall
Frightful, sheer, no-man-fathomed.
                    *Gerard Manley Hopkins*

# ⊠ Contents

# ❸ *Acknowledgements*

Quotations from the work of Bernard Lonergan are made with the permission of the Trustees of the Lonergan Estate, The Lonergan Research Institute, Toronto, Canada. Biblical quotations are generally made from The New Revised Standard Version of the Bible, published by HarperCollins, London. The quotation from Gerard Manley Hopkins at the beginning of the book is taken from *Poems of Gerard Manley Hopkins*, edited by W. H. Gardener (London: Geoffrey Cumberlege/Oxford University Press, 1948), and is quoted by permission of Oxford University Press.

# *Abbreviations*

| | |
|---|---|
| AAS | *Acta Apostolicae Sedis* |
| DS | *Enchiridion symbolorum*, ed. H. Denzinger and A. Schönmetzer |
| DTC | *Dictionnaire de théologie catholique* |
| ND | *The Christian Faith: In the Doctrinal Documents of the Catholic Church*, ed. J. Neuner and J. Dupuis (London: Collins, 1988) |
| NJBC | *The New Jerome Biblical Commentary*, ed. R. Brown, J. Fitzmyer and R. Murphy (London: Chapman, 1990) |
| NRT | *Nouvelle Revue Théologique* |
| par | parallel verses in the other Synoptic Gospels |
| PG | Migne, *Patrologia Graeca* |
| PL | Migne, *Patrologia Latina* |
| RechSR | *Recherches de science religieuse* |
| RJ | *Enchiridion patristicum*, ed. by M. J. Rouet de Journel |
| ST | *Summa Theologica* |
| TI | *Theological Investigations*, in 23 volumes, by K. Rahner (London: Darton, Longman & Todd, 1961–92) |

# ⊠ *Preface*

The flood-tide of books on Christology today never ceases to amaze those familiar with the theological scene, whether the contributions come from exegesis, patristics, spirituality or liberation theology. Mostly these works try to give an overall view of Christ from the perspective of the author's particular speciality. In this book the approach is somewhat different. Here just one aspect of the mystery of Christ – his knowledge and his consciousness – is singled out for attention. It is an aspect which commonly receives some treatment in general books on Christology, but given its central importance, both in Christology in particular and in theology and spirituality generally, it seems appropriate that, in a series entitled *Problems in Theology*, a whole book should be devoted to this topic. It is not a subject which commonly makes headlines in religious controversy today, but it is one which underlies other more widely discussed issues. The nature of revelation in a pluralistic world is a case in point, and even a question like that of women's ordination can be affected by how one estimates the degree to which Christ was a prisoner of the categories of his time.

The title of the book indicates the topic in a general way, but here at the outset a word of caution will be in place: one should not expect too much. If you are hoping to find here a psychology of Jesus, you will be disappointed. Such an account of the interiority of our Saviour is simply not available to us. But the alternative is not total silence either. There are a few points which careful and reflective scholarship can establish with reasonable certitude, and the clarification of these is the goal of this book. Doubtless some will find such a limited outcome not worth the candle. However, even though the reliable fruits of research are not extensive, they are surely of special value in themselves, given the significance of any knowledge of Christ's mind and heart. Then there is also benefit in coming to appreciate the very difficulty of the task itself and why precisely it is hazardous to go beyond such a limited field of affirmation.

Another restriction to be noted from the outset is the fact that this book does not attempt a complete history of the subject-matter, since that would exceed the limits of a series such as this. The author has confined himself to indicating the general lines of such a history and to dealing with a limited number of significant figures, sufficient however to indicate how the problem has developed over the centuries. In such an approach the attention given to the Middle Ages might seem excessive. Certainly an appreciation of this period presupposes a familiarity with scholasticism which is less and less available today. If people have difficulty with that, then they might omit this fifth chapter; but for an understanding of the twentieth-century magisterium in the matter and of recent Catholic theology, some knowledge of the medieval period is essential.

The topic of the eighth chapter of the book brings us before another subject of particular difficulty. Here the precise question is that of consciousness, which, unlike in many other treatments of the matter, this book wishes to distinguish clearly from knowledge. The reasons for this are complex, as indicated in that chapter. Here the author felt obliged to change gear somewhat and to operate at a technical level different from the rest of the book. If one has not got the questions which that chapter is designed to answer, once again the best thing might be to skip the discussion altogether. There is enough in the remainder of the book to interest and satisfy the average reader.

Given the author's own background, the starting-point of the enquiry has been Catholic theology, but Protestant viewpoints have not been neglected. They are present in the chapters on scripture, where the approach is not strictly denominational. They are also treated in the presentation of some outstanding scholars whose positions embody representative currents within English-language Protestant theology.

One of the major difficulties in treating such a topic in any depth is the philosophical aspect, in particular when the subject is consciousness. To an extent it is a problem of the diversity of available opinions, but also there is the difficulty which sometimes arises when such topics are neglected by philosophy altogether. This book cannot wait until such problems have been resolved, and so it makes no apology for taking its place within the field of the philosophy general in Catholic circles, even though here too there is much diversity of opinion. This also gives us a reason for prescinding from one important area of Christ's subjectivity, his freedom. Clearly this aspect would have to be dealt with if the discussion of Christ's interiority were to be truly comprehensive, but the history of the problem shows that the aspect of knowledge and consciousness has been commonly treated on its own. It seems better to leave the profound and difficult question of Christ's freedom to the context of a total Christology rather than to try to treat it here within the limits of this series.

Finally in this preface I would like to express my gratitude to those who helped me in the writing of this book. My thanks go out in a special way to the editor of the series, Michael Walsh, whose invitation sparked off this book in the first place, and whose suggestions on its progress have been much appreciated. I would also wish to thank the librarians of Milltown Park Library, Dublin, for their unfailing courtesy in procuring books at my request.

# 1

⊠ *Questions of method*

No one who undertakes a course of lectures on Christology
will be very long at the task before some member of the
audience will raise the issue of Christ's knowledge and consciousness. The question is formulated in the very title of a
book by the profound Swiss theologian, Hans Urs von
Balthasar, *Does Jesus Know Me? Do We Know Him?*[1] The issue
may be approached from the viewpoint of Christ's knowledge of the world in his present state in heaven, but more
commonly people's interest focuses on what was passing in
Christ's mind and heart during his life on earth. Indeed it is
a question which easily occurs to any devout reader of the
New Testament. One wonders did it occur already to
St Paul, who, if it did, would seem to answer it in the affir-
mative when he speaks of 'the Son of God who loved me,
and gave himself for me' (Gal 2:20).

The question is easily posed; an answer is not so easily
given. The whole issue it raises has been given a central place
in the discussions of Christology down through the centuries. Its importance lies not only in its significance for the
spirituality of the believer, as the statement of St Paul
already suggests, but also, emerging in the course of time as
a crucial issue for theology, it became a test case of where
one stood on the basic dialectic which runs through all
Christology between the unity of personhood and the duality of natures in Christ. As a consequence, when asked this
question in the first few lectures of a course, I personally
always postpone my reply, since such questioners are not yet
in possession of the relevant background for appreciating
the issues in their own question.

The matter has been complicated further by the way it involves one in disputed questions of method. Three main ways of approaching our topic might be described. The first is one which is as widespread as it is unprofessional. It is the approach of those who think that they can answer this question, and many others, simply by looking into their own hearts. I have in mind the religious sister at a renewal course I was giving who argued that she *felt* that Christ must have had doubts and difficulties because *she* had them. It is remarkable that scholars are sometimes less removed from such ingenuous subjectivism than they seem to realize.

Clearly the first principle of any serious pursuit of objectivity in the matter has to be an earnest searching of the scriptures, and this yields a second kind of method which commends itself immediately to many. Here too, however, the process can be falsified from the start by treating the Bible as an independent and self-sufficient norm. This approach can be reinforced by a common contemporary bias towards reading the gospel story in terms of a 'Christology from below', namely one in which the human history of Jesus predominates. It is not too difficult to see that if this should happen, one has already conditioned the outcome of one's reflection by the very choice of method itself.

A third view of method lies in combining scripture and the later tradition of the Church. This approach also is not without its dangers. One can easily fall into an *a priori* way of thinking, which over-emphasizes the divine aspect in Christ and scarcely does justice to the reality of his humanity. At the same time, later tradition cannot be left out of account. Indeed it is the only source of the few points of certainty in an area where so much seems to be a matter of opinion.

The inherent difficulty of the whole question is well summed up in a statement by the Anglican scholar, E. L. Mascall: 'It is indeed both ridiculous and irreverent to ask what it feels like to be God incarnate.'[2] Implicitly this remark is a note of warning, suggesting that the question we are asking can never reach a completely transparent solution. What was in the mind and heart of Christ, and how he viewed the world and its history, will always remain matters shrouded in the mystery which the Son of God is in his very being. At the same time, given that we have some objective knowledge about him, in so far as he is both true God and true human being, given also the manifold data of the New Testament about him, it seems that, by combining scripture and tradition, a few statements can be made as to his knowledge and consciousness with some degree of confidence.

The question can be raised in a twofold perspective: either concerning the knowledge and consciousness which Christ has now as he reigns in heaven, or concerning what passed in the mind and heart of Christ as he walked this earth. In the former perspective, the ordinary believer will be confident enough of the answer. Ever since the early Christians began to call out to the risen one 'Come, Lord Jesus', the whole life of prayer in the Church bears witness to the belief that Christ knows us, knows what we are saying and hears our prayer in a completely individual way. As Son of God, Christ has both his divine knowledge and his human knowledge. Part of the meaning of the glorification of Christ is that his humanity becomes as totally responsive to the divine in him as it is possible for a finite humanity to be. On the level of knowledge, this means that not only is there the Son's divine awareness of each and every individual, but through the beatific vision this awareness overflows into his human mind and heart, so that, both divinely and humanly, he knows and loves each of us.

As regards the second perspective focused on Christ's life on earth, the matter is more difficult. Is there any sense in saying that, prior to his death, Jesus knew me? Some might regard the very question as presumptuous, if not ridiculous, were it not for the fact that, following the suggestion of St Paul (Gal 2:20), such a perspective has been an abiding source of inspiration in the spirituality of the Church.[3] Certainly the way the question of Christ's knowledge has figured in controversy over the centuries has focused on the period prior to his death. The writers generally did not concern themselves with every subsequent individual coming within his horizon in the way to which we have just referred, but they did ask themselves questions concerning how Jesus on earth thought of his death or of the Parousia. This places the problem squarely within the context of his public life, and so the whole issue gets enmeshed in the thorny question of the historical Jesus.

There is no need here to rehearse the well-known story of the oscillation of scholarship on the question of the historical Jesus. From the naive confidence of nineteenth-century historicism, with its biographies of Jesus, the pendulum swung to the opposite extreme with the historical scepticism of Bultmann and his school. In more recent years the pendulum has begun to swing back again, as exegetes have developed sophisticated criteria for sifting the data and strands of gospel tradition.[4] As a consequence it is now at least a valid question to ask whether anything may be affirmed before the bar of historical research concerning the mind and heart of Christ as he went about his life on earth. This will be the focus of the second chapter of this book.

The writers of the New Testament, however, were not historians in the contemporary sense of the term. They were people of faith, telling the story of Jesus in the light of their belief that he was and is the Son of God, now guiding the Church from his place in heaven. In this unique perspective the faith of Christianity was born, to which the Christian Church, indwelt by the Holy Spirit, remains the abiding and providential witness. It is primarily as bearers of this faith of the Church, rather than as simply chroniclers of a remembered experience, that the writers of the New Testament may be questioned as to what they believed about the knowledge and consciousness of Jesus. Obviously this is not a question which they entertained in the comprehensive and systematic way in which it is raised today, but inevitably, in their way of presenting their picture of Christ, their statements can have implications concerning our topic. An approach to our question from this standpoint will be the matter of our third chapter.

The contrast between the two approaches outlined in the last two paragraphs underlines a problem about historical Jesus research which deserves to be explained here more clearly, seeing that the mind of the historical Jesus in particular is a special interest of this book. When people take up their Bibles today, it is always salutary for them to call to mind the considerable distance that separates them from the reality of Jesus' mind which they wish to know better. It is not just a question of the gaps between our time and the writing of the Bible, but rather of the gaps between the Bible itself and the events of which it speaks. We might list five significant aspects or stages in the development of our tradition from the original occurrences it describes to their final appearance in the written text. They are as follows:

1. the actual reality of the mind and heart of Christ in his life on earth;
2. what he wished to reveal by word and deed of that which was in his mind and heart;
3. how all this was grasped by his contemporaries at the time;
4. how they recounted it in the subsequent years of the first century;
5. how their account was set down by the sacred writers in the New Testament.

It is the gaps between these aspects which make the problem of distance so acute. We will now consider these aspects and gaps, one by one, treating them in reverse order. Between the fifth and the fourth there is what might be called the 'redactional' gap, namely that created by the way the sacred writers edited their material in the light of their own ideas and theology. In this process, of course, we believe that they were inspired by the Holy Spirit, but since Vatican II we realize that this charism does not extend beyond the salvific truth of the whole tradition. It can scarcely be claimed that this will guarantee their account in all the details with which we will be concerned. At the same time, the charism of inspiration is not irrelevant to the total picture which is to emerge as to who or what Christ was and is.

The second gap is that between the fourth aspect and the third. It might be described as 'the gap of faith', since it is created by the resurrectional faith of the early disciples, whose account of the original events of Christ's life are so often filtered through their post-Easter understanding. This is the point that lies behind the distinction made above between the second and third chapters of this book.

The third gap, that between the third aspect and the second, brings us up against the misunderstandings, and even

the obtuseness, of the first disciples, for which there is ample
evidence in the gospel story. They themselves admit that
there were points which they understood only in the subsequent period, when their minds went back over the public
life (John 2:22; 12:16). While some of these points were
adverted to later, there must have been many which passed
unnoticed into their memories and were stored there unre-
cognized for being the misrepresentations they were, and so
subsequently distorting the gospel story. Even the apostles
cannot have been immune from the common prejudice that
Jesus' words and deeds corresponded to those which any
ordinary person would have had under the same circumstances. Many of the nuances in what he said and did must
simply have passed over their heads.

The fourth gap is the most impenetrable of all, that
between the face Jesus presented to the world and the inner
mystery which lay behind it all. Jesus of Nazareth was an
enigma to his contemporaries. As time went on, the apostles
seem to have become more conscious of how this enigmatic
quality was grounded in an inner mystery which was simply
beyond them. We can see this situation expressed in the
statement in the Fourth Gospel, 'I have food to eat that you
do not know about' (John 4:32).

Setting out in sequence this list of gaps to be bridged and
difficulties to be overcome, one might well feel tempted once
again to scepticism about saying anything concerning
Christ's knowledge and consciousness during his life on
earth. However, if this review of the difficulties has made
one reluctant to take gospel texts on Christ's knowledge at
their face value, it will have served a purpose. It also pro-
vides a motive for turning to the subsequent tradition of the
Church, to see if from there some light might be found,
which will sustain what from scripture alone can only be
tentative surmise.

This helps to explain why, after considering the New
Testament evidence, this book will then move on to review
how the matter was understood in the subsequent centuries.
After chapters on the intervening periods, the book will
move towards a conclusion with some of the major figures in
twentieth-century Catholic theology. If the method seems
largely descriptive, the underlying intention is definitely

explanatory, for the subject-matter is chosen in order to point towards a solution. With such an important issue and so many major actors in the field, the view of this particular writer can only be as a footnote to the whole story. Though towards the end I will devote some pages to my own view, it will in fact be found to have been conveyed indirectly in the telling of the story and in the choice of material out of which my own view was formed. In particular it will be found in what is common to the three great theologians who figure in Chapter 7 below.

In approaching the solution in this way, I have in mind a certain idea of theological method, inspired by the book of Bernard Lonergan on that topic.[5] To say something about external factors in our Lord's life is one thing; to make some affirmations about his inner mind and heart, and that of a being both human and divine, is quite different. The former kind of statement can be based on historical data. For example, Jesus' death on the cross under Pontius Pilate is as much an historical fact as Caesar's crossing of the Rubicon. But where can we get the data on which to base not just opinions as to what was passing in Christ's mind and heart, but affirmations as to these opinions being true or false? Too much of the discussion of these matters amounts to little more than personal opinions, what Lonergan would call insights and hypotheses. For these the data of the New Testament are a seed-bed of opinion laid out before the enquiring mind of any informed person. But to penetrate beyond such externals to the mind and heart of the God-man, and to aim not just at opinion about him but at truth, is a supernatural act, a function of faith, which must have a basis wider than just the individual enquirer with New Testament in hand. That basis is the life of the Christian community, indwelt by the Holy Spirit, as reflected in its teaching, its theology and its spirituality.

On some basic matters of Christology the Church has given us definitive teaching. As will be explained in a later chapter, these dogmas, though often relevant to our topic, do not answer the precise questions before us. They do give us points of reference and they give a basis of certainty on some issues, which help to raise our discussions above the level of mere speculation; but in the absence of a definitive judgement of the magisterium on the precise topic of this book, we are thrown back on the guidance of the life of the community, on looking at how the matter has been approached by men and women of prayer and in particular by scholars of learning and faith.

I trust that the last few paragraphs will give some insight into the method of this book. With such an elusive and difficult question before us, it cannot be a matter of presenting a neat solution and then drawing a line in the sand. The answer, in so far as one is available to us at all, lies much more at the convergence of a number of probabilities, while large areas of the question must always remain shrouded in mystery. This approach seems to be in line with that of the Pontifical Biblical Commission in its 1981 statement on Christology. It remarked that many exegetes and theologians 'prefer a reverent circumspection before the mystery of his personality. Jesus took no pains to define it precisely, even though through his sayings or deeds he did allow one to catch a mere glimpse of the secrets of his intimate life.'[6]

NOTES

1 Hans Urs von Balthasar, *Does Jesus Know Me? Do We Know Him?* (San Francisco: Ignatius Press, 1983).

2 E. L. Mascall, *Christ, the Christian and the Church* (London: Longmans Green & Co., 1946), p. 37.

3 See already Ignatius of Antioch, 'the cross, through which in his passion he is calling you who are his members', Letter to the Trallians 11 (PG 5:684); see also Letter to the Smyrnaeans 1:1 and 4:2 (PG 5:708 and 709f) and Letter to the Magnesians 5:2 (PG 5:668).

4 E.g. J. P. Meier, *A Marginal Jew*, vol. 1: *The Roots of the Problem and the Person* (New York/London: Doubleday, 1991), pp. 167–84; E. Schillebeeckx, *Jesus: An Experiment in Christology* (London: Collins, 1979), pp. 88–100.

5 B. Lonergan, *Method in Theology* (London: Darton, Longman & Todd, 1972).

6 *Scripture and Christology: A Statement of the Biblical Commission with a Commentary*, edited and commented on by J. Fitzmyer (London: Chapman, 1986), p. 18.

# 2

## ⊠ The preaching of the kingdom

All our questions about Jesus ultimately arise because one day this carpenter of Nazareth turned his back on his shop and his work-bench and took to the roads of Galilee preaching the advent of God's kingdom. This proclamation of the kingdom is commonly accepted as one of the most certain historical facts we have about him. Clearly it tells us something about what was passing in his mind at this stage of his life. The more we can bring into focus the content of that preaching, the more we will be able to form some idea of his inner frame of mind.

There are two aspects of that preaching which are immediately relevant to this task. The first concerns the content of his message and the novelty it represented in the Judaism of his time. The second is the certainty with which he proclaimed it. Leaving aside this second aspect for the moment, we will begin by concentrating on the first.

When our Lord lays down the scroll of Isaiah in the synagogue of Nazareth and says to his relatives and friends, 'Today this scripture has been fulfilled in your hearing' (Luke 4:21), he is presented to us as making one of the key claims of his entire ministry: the kingdom of God is now! The prophets of Israel, and the Jews generally, thought of God's kingdom as belonging to the future. In speaking of the kingdom at all, Jesus sets himself in the same prophetic line, but with his claim that it is already closing in on them, he breaks new ground which, the more one thinks about it, the more revolutionary it appears.

The number of reasonably reliable sayings where this claim may be clearly found are not many,[1] but the key point about them is that they are statements about some of the most characteristic actions of Jesus' ministry – his exorcisms, his meals with sinners, his preaching to the poor; and they interpret these actions as evidence of the kingdom of God as present. In this way the presence of the kingdom can be seen as running through the entire ministry of Jesus. This proclamation of the saving act of God breaking into history is the basic datum on which all New Testament Christology is based.[2]

To the extent that such a datum can be reasonably ascribed to the historical person, it has far-reaching consequences for the knowledge and consciousness of Jesus. It gives us a definite basis on which to develop some picture of his understanding of himself and of his knowledge of God. The contrast with the Baptist is helpful. For the latter this kingdom is close; it is still future but imminent. This represents only a shift of degree in relation to the teaching of the prophets, and it fits in with the apocalyptic currents of the time. In Jesus' case the shift is radical. The reason for urgency is altogether new: the kingdom is here in his own preaching of it, and so ultimately in his own person.

It is commonly maintained that Jesus did not preach himself, and this is true, but only up to a point. It does not seem that he made himself the subject of his discourses. If the Sermon on the Mount is any indication, he spoke rather of the kingdom and of life in the kingdom; but once he began to break away from the tradition of the prophets and to claim the presence of the kingdom in the way he did, he was equivalently making claims about his own task and relationship to God, so that in this indirect way he was preaching himself.

In particular his message had implications for his own knowledge and consciousness, which is the special point of interest here. We might list three such implications as follows. First, it was implied that he had such a knowledge of God and of his will that he knew that God was making an offer of salvation to the world in a way never met with before. Second, he knew that this offer was the final and decisive one by which God would inaugurate his ultimate union with redeemed humanity. Third, he had come to realize that he himself had been singled out by God to be the agent of this extraordinary providence, and that in such a way that this offer by God was being made in Jesus' own word and work. Clearly such a union between his own life and that of God had to rest on a unique grasp of God himself and of him as close.

These implicit claims are clearly extraordinary, and one well may ask for a more specific indication of the evidence for them. One may even wonder whether, at the early stage of which we speak, the kind of language was available at all in which such claims could be formulated. The consensus of scholars about the preaching of the kingdom is surprising, though it still leaves wide room for divergence in the interpretation of the details. One of the clearest texts to which scholars keep returning, and one which demonstrates how the claims we are describing could have been expressed in the language of Jesus, is Matthew 10:32–33 (cf. Luke 12:8–9), where our Lord makes the decision with regard to one's place in the last judgement dependent on one's attitude to his own person: 'Everyone therefore who acknowledges me before others, I also will acknowledge before my Father in heaven; but whoever denies me before others, I also will deny before my Father in heaven.' Here he is equivalently claiming that the final judgement of God is already taking place in his hearers' present response to his preaching.

This same way of seeing his work and person is also conveyed in those sayings in which Jesus is represented as claiming to be the sign of fulfilment: 'Blessed are the eyes that see what you see! For I tell you that many prophets and kings desired to see what you see, but did not see it, and to hear what you hear, but did not hear it' (Luke 10:23–24).[3] 'The queen of the South will rise at the judgment with the people of this generation and condemn them ... something greater than Solomon is here ... something greater than Jonah is here!' (Luke 11:31–32). The same point is implied in the entire healing ministry of Jesus. His miracles mark the undoing of the power of Satan and the onset of God's kingdom: 'But if it is by the finger of God that I cast out the demons, then the kingdom of God has come to you' ( Luke 11:20).[4] In these healing wonders, as in his preaching to the poor, Jesus saw the fulfilment of the prophet's promises of final salvation: 'The blind receive their sight, the lame walk, the lepers are cleansed, the deaf hear, the dead are raised, and the poor have good news brought to them'(Matt 11:5).[5]

Theologians commonly sum up the implications of this evidence by saying that, in the case of Jesus, person and cause are one.[6] Unfortunately this phrase, attractive as it is for its epigrammatic force, can easily lead one astray. Its content is not as precise as one would wish, with the result that it ends in ambiguity. In the light of the evidence which has been discussed, one can certainly give it a meaning already within the limits of fundamental theology. If the coming of the kingdom in Jesus' view depends on his own activity, then person and cause are inevitably in some sense interlocked. But this aspect can be presented in a deeper way, such that it is claimed to contain in germ the whole of classical Christology.[7] This, it seems to me, goes beyond what can be attributed by a responsible exegesis to the historical Jesus. It owes more to reading the New Testament data in the light of subsequent reflection. While this is a perfectly legitimate exercise in the context of systematic theology, I do not think it appropriate to invoke it at the stage of a purely historical consideration of Jesus' public life.

As well as being the eschatological prophet announcing the fact of the coming kingdom, there is also about Jesus of Nazareth something of the traditional teacher in so far as there is some evidence of his giving definitive interpretations of the will of God. In one way this might be seen as placing him in the category of 'rabbi', but it has been pointed out that the very freedom with which he approached the Law of Moses, setting it aside where necessary in favour of his own teaching, separated him radically from the rabbinical schools, for which the authority of Moses was an unchangeable absolute.

For our purposes the interest in this aspect of his teaching lies in the claim to knowledge of God's will which underlies it. In so far as these new interpretations of the law of God were proposed by Jesus, not simply as his own interpretation, but as God's definitive will, they rest on a claim to a unique knowledge of the divine. This also suggests the point that Jesus' special knowledge of God was not just some blinding light of undifferentiated immediacy, but that it included knowledge of particular details of life in this world. It also tells us that the innovations in religious practice which Jesus was proclaiming were not just his own formulae for human living but in certain key respects were discovered by him as flowing from what he had grasped of the nature of God.

One of the most original and striking features of Jesus' teaching was his exclusion of divorce with a view to remarriage: if husbands divorce and remarry, they commit adultery![8] That Jesus should go against so entrenched a position, and that in so intimate and significant a matter, says much for his independence of thought and readiness to challenge the accepted standards of the day. In itself, it cannot be shown that this teaching is anything more than a conclusion of our Lord's human wisdom, but when one bears in mind the prophetic image of divine forgiveness as a model for marriage (Hos 1–3), one can see the teaching as a kind of programmatic sign for the revolutionary teaching on forgiveness which is at the heart of Jesus' gospel.

In some ways even more revolutionary and fundamental is our Lord's teaching on love and forgiveness towards one's enemies. This is a doctrine without parallel in our Lord's world, if not in human wisdom generally. We should notice how the text of Matthew (5:43–48) bases it on an insight into the example of God himself, just as Paul later bases it on the example of Jesus (Rom 5:8–10). Taken by themselves, these texts will seem sporadic, and their authenticity as teaching of the historical Jesus difficult to establish, though the criterion of discontinuity does argue in their favour.[9]

A third aspect of New Testament teaching, which widens the context for the points just made, is the insistence, attributed to our Lord, on the primacy of the human heart. The main occasion for such teaching was our Lord's confrontation with the ritualism of the Pharisees and the tendency of so many of his time to judge only by externals. In this case it was not a question of a teaching totally new. Indeed a similar concern is so clear in the prophets that one wonders how this perspective could have been so commonly lost to view. However few, if any, of the prophets taught it as widely and as radically as did our Lord, with whom it became the vehicle for a whole new approach to interiority, integral to the perfection of the New Testament teaching on God.

In the New Testament we find a view concerning the human condition which belongs so intimately to the entire gospel that it can be argued that it goes back to our Lord himself in some form. Clearly there is something wrong with the world, and people are constantly tempted to isolate their own favourite culprit for this state of things. Social historians will point to the unfair distribution of wealth in the society of the time; the Zealots of the day would point to colonialism, the Pharisees to the people's widespread failure to keep the law. Common to all these recipes is the fact that they deal with external factors. Such factors may indeed have called for reforming, but in our Lord's view of the kingdom what is wrong with the world is something deeper than all these things. He seems to have pointed rather to something within every human being, to the human heart.[10] The external situation of life may indeed need changing, but this is only a symptom of a more fundamental disorder, which arises out of the relationship between human beings and their God. The kingdom Christ is preaching requires a change in the human heart. Certainly the change he is calling for *begins* there. It does not end there, because social relationships are part of the very being of humanity; but it does begin there. To present Christianity as a purely internal religion is a distortion.

Ultimately then Christ's understanding of the human condition was based on the way he understood God. His preaching, says Moltmann, inaugurated a revolution in the concept of God because it broke the old legalism which divided the righteous from sinners.[11] While an appreciation of God's love and mercy for Israel lay at the heart of Jewish faith, the system of reward and punishment that went with it easily translated into a religion of works. Reconciliation was something to be won by human merit on its own rather than to be received from the divine initiative. Mercy was eclipsed by merit and forgiveness by fidelity.

It is clear, however, that central to the New Testament is a different concept of God, one that sweeps away the old image of a divinity to be placated and places at the centre of the religious universe the mystery of divine compassion. For the New Testament the starting-point of the movement of redemption is the God who loves his 'enemies' and forgives them. Reconciliation is not a question of humanity reconciling God to us but of God taking the initiative in reconciling humanity to himself. This is the revolution in the concept of God which lies behind Jesus' revolution in human ethics when he calls on us to put no limit to our forgiveness. All of us are to love our enemies. Even feuding spouses are to forgive rather than to divorce. Though this new concept of religion is worked out more closely in Paul's doctrine of grace, it is also there in the Synoptics, as in Luke's image of the father of the prodigal, or in the implication in Matthew that it is the love of enemies which most makes us resemble God (Matt 5:43–48). If Jesus' new religion is to give a certain primacy to the human heart, that heart is to be, above all, one of compassion and forgiveness.

As well as the fact of the coming of the kingdom and the indications we have just seen as to the nature of the life it brings, one of the most remarkable features of this message of Jesus is the certainty with which he proclaims it. This certainty is conveyed in all kinds of ways, right from the very beginning of his public life. It extends not only to the fact that the kingdom is close but also to the claim that God now wills to revise the Law of Moses in the way proposed by Jesus.

There is one usage which encapsulates this certainty very strikingly. It runs like a refrain through the Sermon on the Mount as Jesus introduces his controversial points to his hearers: 'But I say to you ...' (Matt 5:22, 28, 32, 34, 39, 44). We have to hear that phrase in its context to appreciate the force of its claim. In each case our Lord has just cited a standard tradition about God's will as inculcated by Mosaic precept. The context could not be more solemn, yet Jesus does not hesitate to abrogate and innovate, 'feeling at ease', as one writer put it, 'in a jurisdiction commonly thought to be divine'.[12] Unlike the rabbis he does not appeal to 'what Rabbi X said'; unlike the prophets, he does not claim 'The word of the Lord came to me'. With his solemn refrain, Jesus is expressing his claim to know directly and intuitively what the will of God is now in the new circumstances of the kingdom.[13]

In the instance just cited the claim of authenticity resides more in the thought behind the words than in the words

themselves, but there is an associated usage where the claim
for authenticity can extend even to the very expression itself.
This arises in the phrase 'Amen I say to you ...'. The basis
of the claim in this instance is the fact that the use of 'amen'
as an assertion of certainty *before* a phrase seems to have no
parallel outside its occurrence on the lips of Jesus in the New
Testament. As a result there is considerable support among
exegetes for taking this phrase as one of the rare examples of
an *ipsissimum verbum* of Jesus.[14] Some authors have even
claimed to find in this usage the whole of Christology in
embryo. Certainly it is an important expression of how Jesus
pledges his person behind his message and so, in some
sense, he identifies message, person and cause. Above all
it underlines the certainty with which Jesus viewed his
own message and the conviction with which he possessed it
as the word of God revealed through him. Many of the
instances of this usage occur in the context of the kingdom
or the final judgement, as in Mark 9:1; 14:25 etc. If this can
be accepted, then we have here an actual word of Jesus
expressing the certainty we are attributing to him in his
knowledge of the kingdom.

Equally striking is the fact that this sense of certainty is
attributed to our Lord from the very beginning of his public
life; it seems to continue unwavering throughout his ministry, and it is again attributed to him in the final challenge
before the Sanhedrin. Without having to establish the historical authenticity of each occurrence of this usage, it is
surely remarkable that there is no evidence of any growth in
Jesus' certainty with regard to the central point of his mission. The memory of him that survived in the early Church
was of one who, from beginning to end, proclaimed the
coming of the kingdom with total conviction and uncom-
promising certainty.

One episode in Jesus' life, to which scholars sometimes
refer as a growth point in Jesus' awareness, is his baptism by
John at the Jordan.[15] Apart from the intrinsic difficulty of
saying anything about the historical Jesus on the basis of
gospel texts, one must be careful not to exaggerate the evidence of the texts themselves. It is not impossible that this
event was the occasion for a growth in Jesus' human perception of things from a confused to a more focused idea as

to God's plan for him, but there are simply no grounds in the narrative for psychoanalysing Jesus or for postulating in him a transition from total ignorance about his mission to a new discovery of his destiny. Not a word is said about Jesus' inner experience, nor about any commisssion being laid on him for the first time; and there is a significant silence in the account concerning any inner response of Jesus to the event. The function of the baptismal episode is to establish clearly for the public at large who Jesus is. This is its manifest purpose in the Marcan Gospel, where it is the first major event to be recounted. In Matthew and Luke, where the infancy narratives have already, to an extent, revealed his identity, there is still room for the Jordan narrative to develop the same point further, emphasizing, as it does, Jesus' special relationship to his Father and to the Spirit, as a new stage of his life gets under way.

All this evidence of Christ's revolutionary teaching and of the certainty with which he proclaimed it, inevitably raises in our minds the same question as that attributed to his fellow townspeople, 'Where did this man get all this? What is this wisdom that has been given to him?' (Mark 6:2). Clearly Jesus claims to speak for God. What is more, it is no longer a question of simply continuing a prophetic message about the future but of knowing that, contrary to general expectation, God is about to intervene in the present and bring the whole of history to fulfilment. Such a message, and the certainty with which it is proclaimed, can have their source in only one or other of two alternatives: either it is the creation of a diseased imagination, or it issues from a direct and immediate knowledge of God. Since the first of these alternatives does not fit in with the general evidence of the New Testament, we are left with considering our Lord's relationship to God and the deep and mystic life of prayer with which that relationship was constantly nourished.

The nature of Jesus' relationship to God might at first seem to lie well outside the scope of critical scholarship. Bultmann's scepticism is notorious: 'How things looked in the heart of Jesus I do not know and do not want to know.'[16] However, with the gradual recovery of confidence in the historical study of the gospels, more recent scholarship has focused on the singular use of the word *Abba* as a way for

addressing God in the New Testament, attributed on a few
occasions by the evangelists to Jesus himself. As a result
scholars have come to speak of Jesus' 'Abba experience', and
there is even surprising and significant support for the view
that this way of naming God goes back to Jesus himself.[17] If
this claim can be sustained, it gives us an unexpected and
remarkable insight into something of Jesus' life of prayer. It
implies that he experienced the presence of God in his life
as that of a loving father, with the unique combination of
reverence and intimacy which that term suggests.[18]

One aspect of this discussion concerns the extent to
which this way of addressing God is without parallel in the
Judaism of the time. It is clear that the usage, if found at all
apart from Jesus, is rare, and was not the way God was
addressed in the liturgy of the synagogue. But what is more
significant in the long run, and in itself one of the best sup-
ports for the notion that this usage was characteristic of
Jesus himself, is the way that this mode of address, and the
notion of divinity it implies, encapsulates so perfectly the
revolutionary concept of God and of his will which was set
out earlier in this chapter.

It is a commonplace to observe that Jewish spirituality
generally was marked by a passionate search for the will of
God. Jesus does not depart from this tradition but trans-
poses it into a new key by interpreting it on the model of
filial obedience. This does not entail in any way a surrender
of the ideal of faithfulness, at least where the substantials of
the law are concerned (Matt 23:23), but it does help to bring
about the way the entire life of faith is pervaded by a new
sense of trust, love and boundless forgiveness (Luke 15).
This in turn overflows into a new tenderness for the weak
and the outcast, on the principle that all are children of this
common Father.[19]

Drawing into one the various aspects of the New
Testament which this chapter has been studying, we can say
that they come together in a picture of a Jesus driven by a
unique vision of God.[20] The centre of this vision is the vic-
tory of God's love, overcoming the darkness of this world by
offering forgiveness to all and thereby inaugurating a new
era in human relations. This vision is grasped as so immediate to Christ's person that it is seen as cutting across the long

history of expectation and as already breaking into the course of human affairs. Far from being a figure tortured by self-doubt, such as contemporary prejudice would sometimes wish to see him, the evidence of the New Testament points rather to one in whom the light of his knowledge of God had dispelled all hesitation. The die is cast. The kingdom is now.

This picture of eschatological urgency is transformed into personal drama when one raises the question of Christ's death and of his own attitude to it. Given the difficulties surrounding any consensus about the external details of our Lord's life on earth, to say anything with reasonable confidence about his inner attitude to his own death might seem at first an impossible task. In fact scholarship in recent years has moved away from the blanket scepticism which so influenced an earlier generation of scholars on this issue, and several significant writers have been able to assert a few valuable, if imprecise, points, which fill out our notion of Christ's mind and heart in this important matter.[21]

First of all we might wonder whether our Lord would have thought of a violent end for himself as a possible or likely outcome of the kind of ministry he had undertaken. It seems that after the death of John the Baptist this possibility must have been unavoidable. Then there was the fact that Jesus was commonly understood as being in the line of the prophets of Israel. The martyrdom of such prophets was a standard theme among the people of Christ's day, so that this already sets up an inherent plausibility for the texts that ascribe such a thought to Christ himself, e.g. Luke 13:33. This category has an added interest in that the expiatory nature of such deaths was also a standard theme of the day, a point which already raises the question of what meaning our Lord might have given to his death.[22] The fact that Jesus knew of his approaching end, at the latest by Holy Thursday, and so had to take up some attitude before it, enjoys a surprising degree of support among exegetes today. Into this context we can fit the three main predictions of his death which are found in the synoptic tradition (Mark 8:31 par; 9:31 par; 10:33f par). Exegetes today are not as quick as formerly to dismiss these sayings as simply community creations. While an element of retrojection might be conceded in the details, it is highly unlikely, says Raymond Brown, that none of them stems from Jesus himself.[23]

However, this still does not tell us how our Lord would have understood the significance of his death in relation to his work for God's kingdom. Would he have seen it as frustrating that work, or did he see his death as fitting into, and even furthering, God's plan for the kingdom? Surprisingly, there are just enough indications in the gospels to base a positive answer to that question. The strange phrase comparing his death to a baptism (Mark 10:38f) puts it immediately in an eschatological context and so relative to the coming of the kingdom. That his death, like that of the martyrs generally, would have an expiatory value for the community of the new kingdom is suggested by a saying in Mark 10:45, for which verse a case can be made that it is authentic, at least in its essentials.[24]

Of particular significance for this topic are the eucharistic words of Jesus as handed down in the accounts of the Last Supper. The main text is the eschatological saying in Mark 14:25, which exegetes tend to regard as the verse with the strongest claim to authenticity in these narratives. In refusing to drink the cup until he would drink it new in the kingdom, Jesus combines into one perspective the prospect of his death and the coming of God's reign. If to this we add the phrase 'for you' (Mark 14:24; Luke 22:20), then we can see that the kingdom does not simply follow on his death but is part of the goal of that death. Indeed, in so far as Christ's whole life was one of service for the sake of others, this phrase helps us to see his death as the natural outcome of his life, with both life and death reaching towards continuity in the final reign of God.[25]

It is clear that the post-Easter Church saw even greater depths in the words of the Last Supper, in particular relating our Lord's death and its eucharistic enactment to the fulfilment of the great expiatory sacrifice envisaged in the prophecy of the Suffering Servant. It becomes more problematic if one wishes to establish this as the meaning of the eucharistic words from a purely historical view of the Last Supper; but at least enough has been said to show that a salvific notion of his death has a certain plausibility, even within a purely historical approach to the question.

NOTES

1 Meier, *A Marginal Jew*, vol. 2: *Mentor, Message and Miracles* (New York/London: Doubleday, 1994), pp. 398–454, concentrates on Luke 11:20; Matt 11:5, 11, 12; Mark 1:15. A recent author finds Jesus' claims exclusively in his actions, not in his words: J. C. O'Neill, *Who Did Jesus Think He Was?* (Leiden: Brill, 1997), p. 117.

2 Thus R. H. Fuller, *The Foundations of New Testament Christology* (New York: Scribners, 1965), pp. 130f.

3 For the authenticity of this saying, see Meier, *A Marginal Jew*, vol. 2, pp. 434–9.

4 Cf. Matt 12:28. The statement in Luke 11:20 is one of the key texts for Meier on the kingdom as present: *A Marginal Jew*, vol. 2, pp. 404–30; he also holds for its authenticity, *ibid.*, pp. 413–17. Similarly X. Léon-Dufour, *The Gospels and the Jesus of History* (London: Collins, 1968), p. 230.

5 Cf. Luke 4:16–30. For Old Testament promises, see Isa 35:5f; 29:18f; 61:1.

6 E.g. K. Rahner, *Foundations of Christian Faith* (London: Darton, Longman & Todd, 1978), pp. 251–4; this book is referred to below as *Foundations*. See also W. Pannenberg in *Theology as History*, ed. J. M. Robinson and J. B. Cobb (New York: Harper & Row, 1967), pp. 102–3; W. Kasper, *Jesus the Christ* (London: Burns & Oates, 1976), pp. 100–1.

7 Thus K. Rahner, 'The position of Christology in the Church between exegesis and dogmatics', *Theological Investigations*, vol. XI (London: Darton, Longman & Todd, 1974), pp. 185–214; reference at pp. 201–6. Also Rahner, *Foundations*, pp. 299–302.

8 Following much contemporary scholarship I take the exceptive clause in Matt 5:32; 19:9 as a Matthaean redaction, and the version about wives in Mark 10:12 as also secondary. See J. A. Fitzmyer, *The Gospel according to Luke X–XXIV* (New York: Doubleday, 1985), pp. 1119–24.

9 According to this criterion, texts that cannot be explained by derivation from earlier sources are best explained as original to Jesus: Meier, *A Marginal Jew*, vol. 1, pp. 171–4.

10 For instance, Mark 7:6, 20–21; Luke 6:45; 12:13–21, 30–31 etc.

11 J. Moltmann, *The Crucified God: The Cross of Christ as the Foundation and Criticism of Christian Theology* (London: SCM Press, 1974), p. 142.

12 B. Vawter, *This Man Jesus: An Essay toward a New Testament Christology* (London: Chapman, 1975), p. 139.

13 Thus J. P. Meier, 'Jesus' in *The New Jerome Biblical Commentary*, 78:22.

14 J. Jeremias is especially associated with this view: *New Testament Theology*, vol. 1 (London: SCM Press, 1971), pp. 35–6. See also Meier, *A Marginal Jew*, vol. 2, p. 367, n. 62. The usage may be authentic *in globo*, without necessarily being so in every instance in the gospels. In John's Gospel we find a double 'Amen', which makes

one suspect redactional influence. The statistics of gospel verses where the usage, whether singly or doubled, occurs are: 31 in Matthew, 13 in Mark, 6 in Luke and 25 in John. In the New Revised Standard Version of the Bible, 'Amen' is translated 'truly'.

15 J. D. Dunn, *Jesus and the Spirit: A Study of the Religious and Charismatic Experience of Jesus and the First Christians as Reflected in the New Testament* (London: SCM Press, 1975), pp. 65–6, 85. The view referred to in the text is especially linked to Jeremias' and Cullmann's notion of a revelation at this point to Jesus that the passion of the Servant of Yahweh would be his lot. For this they claim a basis in the Marcan text where the heavenly vision is accorded to Jesus alone.

16 R. Bultmann, *Faith and Understanding* (London: SCM Press, 1969), vol. 1, p. 132.

17 Jeremias, *New Testament Theology*, vol. 1, pp. 61–8; Meier, *A Marginal Jew*, vol. 2, pp. 358–9; 606, n. 31; Fitzmyer, *Luke X–XXIV*, p. 898; R. Brown, *Introduction to New Testament Christology* (London: Chapman, 1994), pp. 86–7.

18 Schillebeeckx, *Jesus*, pp. 256–71; R. Hammerton-Kelly, *Concilium* (3: 1981), pp. 95–102.

19 *Abba* in Aramaic literally means 'the father', but this form was used as a vocative. Contrary to a widespread notion, it is not attested as a child's address to its parent in the period between 200 BC and AD 200, when the form found in that usage was *abi*, meaning 'my father'. Nevertheless the term *abba* certainly implies intimacy. Meier suggests as an English equivalent, 'My dear father', *A Marginal Jew*, vol. 2, p. 294.

20 The word 'vision' here is not yet being used in the technical sense of the immediate vision of God, such as will be found in later chapters.

21 E.g. G. O'Collins, *Christology: A Biblical Historical and Systematic Study of Jesus* (Oxford: Oxford University Press, 1995), pp. 67–80; Kasper, *Jesus the Christ*, pp. 114–19.

22 The expiatory aspect of martyrs' deaths had been spoken of in Israel since Tannaitic times, e.g. 4 Macc 6:28–29; 17:21–22.

23 R. Brown, *The Death of the Messiah: From Gethsemane to the Grave* (New York/London: Doubleday, 1994), vol. 2, p. 1487.

24 This saying 'discloses a basic dimension of the comportment and self-understanding of Jesus ... ,' K. Kertelege, cited by B. Meyer, *The Aims of Jesus* (London: SCM Press, 1979), p. 310, n. 125. See also B. Witherington, *The Christology of Jesus* (Minneapolis: Fortress Press, 1990), pp. 252–4.

25 H. Schürmann, *Comment Jésus a-t-il vécu sa mort?* (Collection 'Lectio Divina' no. 93; Paris: Cerf, 1977), especially pp. 57–81.

# 3

⊠ *Two sets of evidence*

The morning of the resurrection marks a new beginning in his contemporaries' assessment of Jesus of Nazareth. In this study, focused as it is on only one aspect of the reality of Jesus, a certain amount must be assumed as established elsewhere. As already indicated, the discussion we are conducting takes its stand more or less at the centre of contemporary scholarship. This means that here the reality of the resurrection, as something that happened to Jesus, and not just to his disciples, is assumed. We must also take as historical the great change which the New Testament sees coming over the disciples as the truth of Christ's resurrection is borne in on them. This transformation is, as one exegete put it, 'a stunning phenomenon',[1] and the subsequent achievement of the disciples in the spreading of the Christian message is one of the best historical arguments for the reality of their claims. The coming into being of the primitive Christian movement 'rips a great hole in history ... a hole the size of the resurrection'.[2]

The event of the resurrection also marks a new stage in the development of Christian faith. Faith in his person had always been something which Jesus had been concerned to solicit, nurture and confirm. But it is one thing to believe in Jesus as a human messenger from God; it is another to see him as the Son of the Father, thereby making himself equal to God (John 5:18). While we can never be sure precisely as to the moment when the first disciples began to move from the former to the latter assessment of Jesus, the transition is so profound and paradoxical, not least in a society proud of its monotheism, that it seems reasonable to expect that it could come about only within the context of some shattering experience of divine power. The resurrection appearances of Christ must have constituted just such an experience, as indeed the confusion and hesitation in the gospel narratives suggest, so that it seems reasonable to postulate that it was only on the crest of their experience of the risen Christ that the disciples came to this transcendent faith. Whenever it happened, it certainly represents the mature belief of the New Testament churches, a belief that casts a new light on the entire story of Jesus.

Consoling as this is for the believer, then and now, it leaves us with the historian's well-known difficulty, to which reference was made in the opening chapter. The whole New Testament story is told in the light of this transcendent faith in the risen Lord, with the result that it is only with the greatest difficulty that authentic records of the historical Jesus can be disentangled from memories inflated with post-resurrection belief. Various methods have been devised for dealing with this problem. In the preceding chapter we grasped the nettle of the difficulty and attempted to isolate a few items of information which historians might be invited to accept. In this chapter the method will be to begin by accepting the fact of resurrection faith. We will then set out further data on Christ's knowledge from the New Testament, prescinding from the historical value of particular texts, content to reflect on the many-faceted image of Christ which lived on in the believing memory of the New Testament writers. The important thing for us now is to focus on who or what they believed Jesus Christ to be. Whether this came home to them before or after the resurrection is a secondary matter.

Surveying the image of Christ in the context of the New Testament means that we begin to reflect on our basic question out of that experience of the risen Lord which began with the birth of the Church and continues on into our own world and beyond. Whatever answer one gives to any question about Christ can be formulated in a reliable manner only from within the way the Christian Church has experienced him. The first stage of this experience is that represented by the New Testament itself. It is then with this sense of some providential continuity between their church life

and ours that we turn in this chapter to the New Testament
writers to question them on the subject which concerns us.

The central fact about Christ's knowledge, which these
writers put before us, is a conflicting picture, summed up in
the way the relevant evidence soon divides into two contrasting sets of texts. On the one hand there is a series of
statements suggesting limitations of Christ's knowledge. On
the other there is a further series suggesting hidden depths
in his knowledge. When viewed from the perspective of later
language in the Church, we can interpret this contrasting
picture as a manifestation of a much deeper distinction within the mystery of Christ, namely the distinction without sep-
aration between real humanity and real divinity in him.

### Limitations in Christ's knowledge

We might begin with the infancy narrative in Luke's Gospel,
where Jesus is said to grow in wisdom, age and grace (Luke
2:52). If Jesus really grew in wisdom and the knowledge it
implies, then at least at the earlier stages of his life he was
without the knowledge and wisdom which he later acquired.
This gives us a picture of a normal growing boy, gradually
acquiring the various skills he will need in life, learning to
read, gaining the knowledge and the craft which his trade as
a carpenter requires, growing in his understanding of the
ways of the world.

Sometimes in the gospels there are incidental remarks
which seem to throw special light on the topic we are studying. There is, for instance, the surprise with which our Lord
is said to respond to the unbelief of his fellow townspeople
(Mark 6:6). Such a reaction implies that this was something
which he had not known before and was not expecting. That
such a response was later seen as problematic, once the full
faith in his divinity had emerged, is underlined by the way
Matthew's Gospel eliminates it from his version of the same
story (Matt 13:58). Such details also tend to be eliminated in
John's Gospel.[3] Modern commentators commonly go on to
assume that the situation alleged by Mark is historical, and
that of Matthew is simply redactional. While this may indeed
be the case, such an assumption can point to a certain presupposition on the part of the commentator. The basis of the

evidence is surely too narrow and the point too insignificant for us to decide the historical question with any degree of certainty.

In general, in considering evidence for Christ's lack of knowledge, it will be useful to distinguish between points that touch on the major concerns of Christ's mission and points that are merely incidental. As examples of the latter, there are a number of texts in which Christ is represented as going along with the standard ideas of his time, ideas which we would now consider mistaken. Some of these are medical points, as when the condition which we would diagnose as simply epilepsy is treated as a case of demonic possession (Mark 9:23–24).[4] Some are exegetical points, as when the Davidic authorship of the psalms is taken as authentic (Mark 12:35–37).[5] It is of course an open question with what certainty these points may be attributed to the historical Jesus, but if we assume that he did indeed act and speak in these terms, this still tells us nothing more about him than that he wished to be a man of his time. In the perspective of his mission to save the world, such details are only incidental. It cannot be ruled out that he would have accepted such ideas simply as a manner of speaking, even while knowing them to be wrong, as long as it was not part of his mission to get involved in such questions;[6] or, as is more likely, he simply took them over from his contemporaries without questioning them on the level of his explicit knowledge.[7]

There are, however, two pieces of evidence as to Jesus' lack of knowledge which are of a more serious nature, since they concern a matter that is right at the heart of Jesus' understanding of his mission. The first concerns the statement in Mark 13:32 that Jesus does not know when the day of judgement is to come. The second goes even further and suggests that Jesus was in actual error on the point by his apparent assumption that the event could not be far distant. It is one thing if the agent of revelation is in the dark as to the climax of his story; it is even more embarrassing if he seems to claim knowledge of the same point and is then found to have been in error. In responding to these two difficulties we will begin with the second and with the three relevant texts: Matthew 10:23, Mark 9:1 and Mark 13:30.

Among the many sayings attributed to Jesus which

suggest an imminent arrival of the kingdom of God, what gives particular relief to the three we are now studying is the way they seem to come down on the side of a particular timetable for the event, namely within a generation in the case of Mark, and before the conclusion of the mission to Israel in the case of Matthew. Clearly that is not the way it turned out. Hence the problem.

Common to all those who see evidence in these texts for an error on Jesus' part is the opinion that these verses, at least substantially, are authentic sayings of Jesus. This opinion, however, has never been universal – being rejected already by Bultmann in his *History of the Synoptic Tradition*.[8] More recently J. P. Meier has called it into question once again.[9] Meier argues that these sayings are creations of the post-Easter community, reflecting the way the early Church conceived the imminence of the kingdom rather than the way it was understood by Jesus himself. Their origin may be due to words of comfort pronounced by early Christian prophets, as Meier postulates, or they could initially be statements about the fall of Jerusalem, authentic or otherwise, which were later reshaped into being statements about an imminent Parousia. Either way, they are not acceptable evidence for attributing error to Jesus in such a major matter, unless that is the kind of Christology one has already assumed.[10]

The problem posed by Mark 13:32 is more difficult. It is one of the most paradoxical statements attributed to Jesus in the New Testament. Taking it at its face value, it is, on the one hand, evidence of a 'low Christology' with its assertion of Jesus' lack of knowledge; on the other hand, by referring to Jesus as 'the Son', it points rather towards a 'high Christology', analogous to the kind of viewpoint we associate with the Fourth Gospel. The first question that exegetes will want to decide is that of its authenticity. Here, as one might expect, opinions divide; but the reasons for taking it as authentic, at least in its essentials, are serious, so that the systematic theologian would be well advised to act on that assumption.[11]

To assign a timetable for the Parousia was a characteristic of apocalyptic, and from this movement the tendency seems to have passed into some circles among the early Christians (cf. 1 Thess 4:13–18; 1 Cor 15:51–53). This concern was in marked contrast with that found in the Old Testament and continued, as far as we can judge, in the preaching of the Baptist. In this more traditional view there was a vagueness about the *when* of the Parousia. The question for us is whether Jesus was closer to the apocalypticists, as Matthew 10:23, Mark 9:1 and 13:30 suggest, or whether Mark 13:32, with its emphasis on the unknowability of the Parousia, reflects his actual teaching and approach. As Meier has brought out so well, verses 30 and 32 in Mark 13 cannot both be authentic, at least if one takes them literally.[12]

The weight of the argument, both exegetically and theologically, favours the substantial authenticity of Mark 13:32. There is an intrinsic plausibility in the notion that Jesus insisted on an imminent but ultimately incalculable Parousia. Such a doctrine calls forth immediately a far-ranging spiritual attitude of unremitting vigilance, which fits in with a number of other passages in the New Testament.[13] It also opens out the teaching of the gospel to the notion that the finality of judgement is not only present in the calamities of every age, from the fall of Jerusalem in AD 70 to the fall of Berlin in our own century; it is also present in the awesome irreversibility of the moment of death for each individual.

Taking Mark 13:32 then as an authentic statement of lack of knowledge on Jesus' part, various modes of interpretation have been devised by the ingenuity of scholars for dealing with it, but the most important one is the most straightforward: Jesus was simply ignorant of the date of the Parousia, as ignorant, some would add, as you or I. A more devious approach is that of some older scholastics, namely that Jesus had knowledge of the Parousia clearly within his express human knowledge but withheld it out of obedience to the Father. Equivalently he was saying that he had no communicable knowledge; it was not part of his function to give such information (cf. Acts 1:7), just as in Matthew 20:23 he says that he has no function in assigning rewards. A more subtle version of the same position is the view that, because it was not part of Christ's mission to reveal such matters, the timing of the Parousia was not present to him clearly on the level of express human knowledge. This leaves open the possibility that it was present to him on some other level of knowledge in a manner beyond our comprehension, but not as part of what can ordinarily be expressed in human speech.

Later in this book a theory of levels in Christ's knowledge will be pursued, but in the meantime it seems best to confine oneself to taking Mark 13:32 as it stands, namely as evidence of a level in him characterized by ignorance of the date of the Parousia. What we must guard against, however, from the outset is the temptation to conclude that, in respect of knowledge and ignorance, Jesus was no different from any other human being. That may have been the assumption of those who first heard these words of Jesus and handed them down to us, but that cannot be a presupposition for our interpretation of this text, given all the other things we now know about this unique and mysterious person. Indeed, even in this text itself, there is a hint of this deeper reality in the unique relationship between Jesus and God suggested by the absolute use of 'the Son' and 'the Father'.

### Hidden depths

Having seen the evidence for limitations in Christ's knowledge, we must now consider a contrary series of passages, where it is indicated that there are hidden depths in that knowledge, depths we can only guess at. The initial evidence for this has already been given when we studied our Lord's certainty in the proclamation of the kingdom, a characteristic all the more remarkable for being established within a purely historical consideration. In this chapter the same point will be filled out from passages of the New Testament where the historical question has to be set aside. Here we consider how our Lord was understood in the post-resurrection faith of the early Christians. The image of Christ which thus emerges is always evidence for who and what Jesus is believed to be in the Church, though that still leaves an open question as to the extent to which his identity was already influencing his activity in the precise way and at the precise time in which it is said to occur in the gospel narratives.

In this context the place of the Fourth Gospel is particularly problematic. It is clear that this gospel attributes hidden depths to Christ's knowledge. These attributes are certainly evidence as to how Jesus' identity was conceived by the early Church. They cannot, of course, be taken as evidence of the way Jesus was spoken of, either by himself or by others, during his public life. As to what Jesus *was* at that time, or as to what was passing in his mind at that period, that is another matter. Certainly such statements cannot be taken literally as evidence of what was happening explicitly in Jesus' human knowledge at the period of which they are asserted by the gospel. Nevertheless, in so far as they are evidence of Jesus' identity, and that identity, as we will see, is the permanent condition of his *being* at all times, these assertions cannot be considered totally irrelevant. They are a constant reminder to us that Jesus of Nazareth can well be more than he at first seems.

As regards the Fourth Gospel, it is also necessary to bear in mind that its basic thrust receives some confirmation in the synoptic picture of Jesus as described in the preceding chapter. Here we recall briefly how we saw Jesus' *Abba* experience at the centre of his life and thought. It must have been from this insight into God, communicated to him in this experience, that he articulated for us his revolutionary conviction about the divine compassion and the new life of universal concern and forgiveness which it called for among believers. But underpinning this vision of a world reborn, his insight into God also grounded his unwavering certainty as to the closeness of the kingdom and the definitive place which the Father had given him within it. Once this is accepted as historically based, then one has to view the Fourth Gospel, not as creating the image of Christ's transcendence out of the air, but rather as developing and deepening what was already outlined in germ in the Synoptics.

Knowledge and consciousness are based on being. What Jesus knows of himself, of God and of the world depends on who and what he is. While the question of Jesus' identity was certainly raised during his life on earth, the definitive answer as to his divine sonship seems to have come, as was suggested above, only as a result of his resurrection.[14] Attempts to find this belief fully explicit in the period before Christ's death simply underestimate the problems involved. On the one hand there was a problem of faith. The whole history of

Israel had been centred on the proud proclamation of God's oneness as against a polytheistic paganism.

In addition there was a difficulty of language. If Jesus were to walk into the synagogue of Nazareth and announce to his townspeople 'I am God', the statement would be, not only shocking, but, at least as they would hear it, false. It would be as if he said 'I am the Father', since at that stage 'God' and 'Father' were synonymous. Before such truths could be revealed, and before the language to express them had evolved, some time had to elapse. It seems reasonable to claim in addition that some profoundly disturbing experience had to intervene to open the disciples up to the possibility that the old world and its categories were no more and that they had to think in a totally new way. The resurrection of Jesus, as has already been remarked, was just the event to bring this about.

Of the many titles given to our Lord in the New Testament, one of the most helpful for naming his identity is that of 'Son of God'. As regards this title, some of the problems just referred to return in some detail. The notion behind this title has some basis in Israel in the way the king was regarded as God's son in 2 Samuel 7:14 and in Psalm 2:7, but this was a strictly functional and metaphorical use of the notion. It designated the king simply in his function as providential ruler. In no way did it designate the being of the king. The most we could say is that he was God's son by adoption. Given this weak background, it is perhaps not surprising that the title 'Son of God' was not in general currency for the Messiah prior to the New Testament, though it may have been just beginning to enter use in Jesus' time.[15]

Though the title is commonly applied to our Lord in the New Testament, and that even in the setting of his public life (e.g. Matt 16:16), scholars today will commonly see such usage as redactional. There is no clear evidence for the use of this title by our Lord himself. In this context a remark of Pierre Benoit many years ago still seems appropriate:

> Jesus never said outright, 'I am the Son of God.' It
> was something he simply could not say at a time
> when a statement of this kind could never be under-
> stood in its true sense. But he did better. He revealed
> a union between himself and God his Father so

singular and transcendent that it had the effect of
placing him on the same divine level as the Father.
This is the force of those statements in which he
claimed to be not only a son but 'the Son.'[16]

Certainly when the first Christians came to put into
words the unique relationship between Jesus and God, one
of the principal modes of expression that came to them was
that of the relationship between Son and Father. Inevitably
this must have had functional overtones at first, but as the
New Testament tradition developed, one can trace the growing emphasis on the possible ontological implications of the
language as the terms were filled out with new content. The
concept of the virgin birth and that of Christ's pre-existence
certainly had a role to play, but the fundamental step forwards surely came out of the realization that the future kingdom of God was already in some sense present in this person who had risen from the dead. Whatever the details of
this development – and each stage of the process will pro-
vide scholars with a battleground – it is clear that by the time
of the Fourth Gospel, if not before, the Church understood
Christ's sonship as implying his equality with the Father.[17]

This establishment of our Lord's identity by the early
Church is crucial for an understanding of Jesus' consciousness and knowledge. Once one accepts from the Church
that Jesus really is a divine person, equal to the Father – a
notion eventually expressed in the New Testament by the
title 'Son of God' – then one must face up to the fact that
his divinity, in the absolute sense of the Judeo-Christian tradition, is not something he can acquire or grow into.[18] One
might paraphrase John 1:14 by saying 'God became man',
but the obverse can never be true, 'A man became God'.
Consequently, if Jesus was Son of God after the resurrection, he was also Son of God before it, though the way this
was manifested in his humanity may have been different
before and after his death.

Furthermore, divinity implies consciousness. The notion
of divinity in a state of suspended consciousness is an
impossible one in the Judeo-Christian tradition about God.
It follows therefore from the New Testament's identifying
Jesus as Son of God that, while on earth, he was conscious
of this unique divine relationship between himself and the

deity. However, we have very little information as to how he expressed that relationship to himself, but we do have his designation of God as *Abba*, Father, which makes it almost unavoidable that he understood his own position in some such filial terms as were later attributed to him in the Fourth Gospel.[19]

Of particular interest is the way the Fourth Gospel has developed language capable of putting into words the profound idea we are examining. The clearest mode of expression lies in the series of solemn 'I am' sayings (Greek: *ego eimi*) with which the Johannine Christ is presented as manifesting an awareness of his own divinity.[20] We may wish, as has been suggested,[21] to interpret this as indicating a *human* awareness of a divine *ego*, but to maintain this with any confidence is already to rely on refinements from a later theology in the reading of the text. The main point is surely the fact that the faith of the early community had already gone so far in its appreciation of Christ's inner mystery and had already found the language to present it in such challenging terms to later generations.

It is against this background that one should approach the actual statements in the New Testament about Christ's special knowledge. Prophets in Israel were commonly understood to be granted from God special illuminations concerning their task, for instance the kind of knowledge referred to in Luke 7:39. This is what the theological tradition would later call 'infused knowledge'. Once Christ is seen to be in the line of the prophets, it is only to be expected that gifts of special knowledge should be attributed to him. Statements in the gospels about Christ knowing what is in the hearts of the bystanders can be seen in this light.[22] Also relevant are statements about Christ knowing things at a distance.[23] While the ultimate evaluation of such statements, whether from an historical or a theological point of view, has to remain open, the fact is that, even as they stand, they manifest an image of Christ which sets him apart from the ordinary.[24]

A further text pointing in the same direction comes up in a context where one would not expect it. Paul's references to Jesus in his life on earth are notoriously sparse. This makes all the more surprising his statement in Galatians 2:20 that

Christ loved Paul and gave himself up for the apostle. This is a statement about Jesus before his death, at a time when, as far as we know, Jesus had not met Saul of Tarsus and, humanly speaking, did not know him. In itself the statement is capable of many interpretations. Commonly, exegetes will prefer to take Paul's first person singular here in a typical sense, standing for people generally, rather than as applying to Paul himself as an individual.[25] However, no matter how the verse is to be understood eventually, certainly it deserves to be added to our list of relevant texts, at least in a preliminary way, since its most literal meaning attributes some kind of special knowledge to Jesus before his death.

A stronger basis belongs to the special knowledge attributed to Christ in his role as bearer of a new revelation from God. This point is brought out in one of the most famous and impressive texts in the gospels, which is all the more remarkable for being found early on in the synoptic tradition: Matthew 11:25–27 and Luke 10:21–22. These verses clearly designate Jesus as revealer. The knowledge of God which they attribute to him is put forward on the basis of a unique relationship between himself and the Father, and the significance of this relationship is in turn deepened by the description of the knowledge which it makes possible. According to the text itself, this knowledge is immediate, exclusive and, above all, reciprocal. The equality this implies helps to confirm the suggestion, already contained in the designations 'the Son', 'the Father', that this relationship is based on an equality of being. As the commentaries commonly agree, this text anticipates, already in the Q tradition, a view of Christ, and specifically of him as revealer, which is later developed and expanded in the Fourth Gospel, where the aspect of immediacy between Jesus and the Father is given even greater emphasis.[26]

Such explicit emphasis on Christ as revealer is to be contrasted with the striking fact that nowhere in the New Testament is our Lord referred to categorically as a 'believer'. This fact of the tradition must stand out as a headline for any further discussion, which certainly is not thereby ruled out, as to whether Christ had faith, and, if so, to what extent. This topic will be treated later on in this book in the context of the more developed systematic theology which it requires. Certainly the point cannot be decided by the few incidental passages to which scholars sometimes appeal – one suspects out of prior theological assumptions. For instance, the statement in Hebrews 12:2 that Jesus is the 'author and finisher' of faith is the text most frequently brought forward in this context.[27] Some have appealed to Mark 9:23-24 on the basis that Jesus cannot hold up faith as an ideal unless he himself practises it.[28] Texts in Paul which may be translated 'the faith of Jesus' have also been invoked, but there is no consensus about taking this genitive as subjective in the way the argument would require.[29] Surely these texts are tenuous and unconvincing when set beside the general picture of Jesus as revealer which has just been described.

This completes our survey of the relevant New Testament data on the knowledge attributed to Christ. As was pointed out at the outset of this enquiry, this evidence breaks up into two contrasting sets of texts, those that indicate limitations in his knowledge and those that suggest hidden depths of insight within him. It is not immediately obvious how both these sets of texts can be reconciled within one person.

The first point that emerges from this fact is that, in the debates about the fullness or the limitations of Christ's knowledge, the witness of scripture is not unambiguously on the one side or the other. In traditional scholasticism the image of an all-knowing Christ has predominated. In more recent writing, largely as a result of the biblical renewal, many theologians have conveyed the impression that a stumbling, doubting, searching Christ was required by the New Testament. In fact our survey establishes that the reality is far from being so straightforward, and that the overall evidence of the New Testament remains ambiguous and inconclusive. Indeed this is the last issue one should try to settle on the basis of scripture alone. It is a prime example of a question where scripture needs the help of the dogmatic tradition to decide. In fact our topic is but an aspect of the fundamental problem of all Christology as to how the fullness of humanity and the fullness of divinity can come together within the one being.

NOTES

1  Meyer, *Aims of Jesus*, p. 60.
2  C. F. D. Moule, *The Phenomenon of the New Testament* (London: SCM Press, 1967), p. 1.
3  For another example of this process at work, contrast Mark 11:13 with Matt 21:19.
4  Meier, *A Marginal Jew*, vol. 2, p. 655. It is worth noting that many exegetes today consider that the historical Jesus actually performed exorcisms, e.g. Meier, *ibid.*, p. 969.
5  Similar to this case are the errors of fact attributed to Jesus in Mark 2:26; Matt 23:35, as the standard commentators explain.
6  If one thinks such an attitude incompatible with the Jesus of the gospels, one might bear in mind a certain lack of candour attributed to him by the gospels themselves as the occasion required it (Luke 24:19; John 7:8–10).
7  Exegetes sometimes invoke as further incidental evidence of Christ's lack of knowledge texts in which he is represented as asking questions in order to learn something, e.g. Mark 6:38; 11:13; Luke 8:30. Because of the historical difficulties surrounding such texts, I omit them here, though the picture they suggest will be seen to be ultimately compatible with the position of this book.
8  R. Bultmann, *History of the Synoptic Tradition* (Oxford: Basil Blackwell, 1963), pp. 121–7.
9  Meier, *A Marginal Jew*, vol. 2, pp. 336–48. An alternative approach to the question of error on Jesus' part, assuming the authenticity of Mark 9:1, and somewhat similar to the solution proposed by Rahner in Chapter 7 below, will be found in A. E. Harvey, *Jesus and the Constraints of History* (Westminster: The Philadelphia Press, 1982), pp. 86–97.
10  The consensus of older scholars concerning an apocalyptic Jesus preaching the end of the world has been considerably eroded in recent times. Thus Marcus Borg argues that the 'coming Son of Man sayings', of which Matt 10:23 is one, are to be viewed as inauthentic, and these were the primary foundation of the hypothesis of an eschatological Jesus: M. Borg, *Jesus in Contemporary Scholarship* (Valley Forge: Trinity International, 1994), p. 51.
11  See, for instance, the discussion in Meier, *A Marginal Jew*, vol. 2, p. 347.
12  *Ibid.*, p. 347.
13  Matt 24: 45–51; 25:1–13; Luke 12:16–21. Cf. 1 Cor 7:29–31.
14  Texts in which this seems to be implied would be: Rom 1:3f; Eph 1:20; Phil 2:9–11; 1 Pet 3:21f; Acts 13:33; John 14:20. Some would also see it as the significance of the title 'Lord' in texts such as Acts 2:32, 36; Luke 24:34; John 20:18, 25; 21:7. On this matter see Schillebeeckx, *Christ: The Christian Experience in the Modern World*, (London: SCM Press, 1980), p. 252; Kasper, *Jesus the Christ*, p. 149.
15  Qumran 4 Q Flor. 10–14; 1 Q Sa. II 11f; 4 Q ps Dan Aa. See Brown, *Introduction to New Testament Christology*, p. 81; Dunn, *Jesus and the*

*Spirit*, p. 371, n. 156. As regards the articulation of Jesus' claim in terms of the Messiah, the standard authors may be consulted, e.g. Brown, *Introduction to New Testament Christology*, pp. 73–80. The recent emphatic statement of this Messianic aspect by O'Neill, *Who Did Jesus Think He Was?*, pp. 115–35, has been rightly criticized for not doing justice to the development of concepts within the gospel tradition.

16  P. Benoit in *Son and Saviour: The Divinity of Jesus Christ in the Scriptures*, ed. A. Gelin (London: Chapman, 1965), p. 77. The application to himself of the term 'son' is at least implicit in Jesus' calling God 'Abba', even if he did not apply to himself explicitly the title 'the Son'.

17  A similar outcome could be reached by studying the application of the title 'Lord' to Jesus. For this, the standard authors may be consulted: B. Vawter, *This Man Jesus*, pp. 99–104; Fuller, *Foundations*, pp. 156–8, 184–6; O'Collins, *Christology*, pp. 136–42.

18  The situation would be different where divinity is not understood as the absolute possession of the fullness of being, such as in Hellenistic religion.

19  For an example of an exegete attempting to fill out this claim scripturally, see A. Feuillet, 'Les Ego Eimi christologiques du quatrième évangile', RechSR 54 (1966), pp. 5–22, but note also the discussion of this exegete's views in J. Galot, 'Le Christ terrestre et la vision', *Gregorianum* 67 (1986), pp. 429–50.

20  Here I refer especially to the absolute use of this expression as in John 8:58. See also John 6:20; 8:24, 28; 13:19; 18:5, 8. Cf. Mark 6:50; 14:62. Of these Johannine verses, John 8:58 is the most striking and explicit. The principal background for such sayings is found in prophetic texts such as Isa 43:10, 13; 45:18; 46:4; 48:12.

21  Galot 'Le Christ', p. 438. Galot's approach to consciousness will be discussed below in Chapter 8.

22  Mark 2:6–8; 9:33–34; Luke 9:46–47; John 2:24–25; 16:19, 30.

23  Mark 11:2; 14:13–14; Matt 17:24–27; Luke 22:10; John 1:48–49.

24  The historical question concerns whether such statements are only redactional or are authentic memories of the historical Jesus. On the latter assumption there remains the theological question as to whether these are instances simply of Christ's natural perceptiveness, or do they rather represent evidence of supernatural knowledge.

25  H. Schlier, *Der Brief and die Galater* (Gottingen: Vandenhoeck and Ruprecht, 1951), p. 59; J. D. G. Dunn, *The Theology of Paul's Letter to the Galatians* (Cambridge: Cambridge University Press, 1993), p. 54.

26  John 1:14, 16, 18; 3:11, 31–36; 5:19–20; 6:46; 8:26, 28, 38, 54–55; 10:15; 12:50; 17:8.

27  The Greek reads *archègos kai teleiôtes*. The translation in the text is that of the Douay version.

28  This aspect is discussed by Meier, *A Marginal Jew*, vol. 2, p. 655.

29  See Gal 2:16; Rom 3:21 and 26. Fitzmyer takes the genitive as objective meaning 'faith in Jesus': NJBC, paras 47:19; 51:38. See also Dunn, *Galatians*, pp. 57–8.

## 4

⊠ *The patristic era*

The centuries of the patristic era are the time when the great movements concerning Christ's humanity and his divinity were sweeping over the Church. In these centuries of division and uncertainty the pendulum of theological opinion swung backwards and forwards, sometimes bringing out the reality of Christ's humanity, sometimes that of his divinity. In the ebb and flow of controversy, the question of Christ's knowledge figured from time to time with varying degrees of emphasis. In fact, as the great issue between Christ's divinity and the reality of his humanity was being resolved, the ground was being prepared for some reconciliation of the two sides of the contrast we have seen in the New Testament between the limitations of Christ's knowledge and its hidden depths.

### The second and third centuries

For our topic we can divide the patristic era into four main periods, and the first of these arises among the writers who follow immediately on the New Testament. This is a world very different from our own. Our natural inclination is to take Christ's humanity for granted and to have problems about his divinity. In the time of which we speak the reverse seems to have been the case. A common movement of thought, often of a Gnostic tendency, seems to have taken the transcendent assessment of Christ for granted, but found the reality of his humanity problematic. This was the time of *docetism*, which held that Christ only *appeared* (Greek: *dokein*) to live in the flesh but was really a spirit in disguise. This tendency was resisted by the orthodox, and we find writers like Irenaeus (*c*.130–*c*.202) and Origen (*c*.185–253) appealing to Christ's lack of knowledge in Mark 13:32 as evidence of the reality of his humanity.[1] In this early period, however, one has to say that the references to Christ's lack of knowledge are only incidental.

## *The struggle with Arianism and Apollinarianism*

The issue became more central in the second of our four periods, when the controversy with Arianism was at its height. Working on the assumption of Christ's unity of being, the Arians gladly seized on evidence for his ignorance as an argument for the finitude of the heavenly Word. Athanasius' reply was a distinction between Christ as human and Christ as divine. 'As God' or 'as the Word' he knew, but 'as a human being' he did not know.[2] Athanasius frequently acknowledged, as in the passage just referred to, that 'ignorance is characteristic of a human being', and so he conceded that there were things of which 'as man' Jesus was ignorant, such as the day of the Last Judgement. At the same time, however, he insisted that 'as God' there was nothing Jesus did not know.[3] Here we see emerging a tendency, which will only grow in significance throughout the subsequent period whenever questions of Christ's knowledge or lack of it are raised: a concern to vindicate the reality of his divinity, and so to assert the dominance of his divine knowledge, tends to outweigh everything else. It is this which ultimately determines the issue, with the result that intimations of ignorance are eventually eclipsed by the reality of divine knowledge in Christ.[4]

Just as a tradition was beginning to form around the insistence on Christ's divine knowledge, the pendulum suddenly began to swing in the opposite direction with the emergence of Apollinarianism. This heresy was an exaggeration on the side of Christ's divinity. According to Apollinaris, so dominant was the reality of Christ's divinity and of the divine knowledge that went with it, that any presence of a rational, finite soul in Christ would have been superfluous. Reactions to this position brought attention to bear directly on evidence for Christ's human knowledge as a manifestation of his finite soul. Gregory of Nazianzen remarked that it would be madness to place one's hopes in a man lacking a human mind.[5] Authors like Gregory appeal precisely to Mark 13:32 to support their case against Apollinaris.[6] This aspect was reconciled with the thesis of Christ's divine wisdom by the distinction 'as human' – 'as divine' in the manner described in the preceding paragraph. Ambrose is a good example of a writer caught between Arianism and Apollinarianism. Against the Arians he argues that Christ knew about the last day and did not wish to reveal it.[7] Against the Apollinarians he points to Luke 2:52 as evidence that Christ had to grow in knowledge.[8]

### The struggle with Nestorianism

Though in this way the controversies of the second in our four periods had already given a central place to questions of Christ's knowledge, it was really only in the third period, in reaction to the rise of Nestorianism, that some of the crucial issues behind the question of knowledge were finally laid bare.[9] Ever since the rise of Apollinarianism, Antiochene theology had been stressing the evidence for real ignorance and real development in Christ.[10] On the other side of the debate from the Antiochenes the dominant figure was of course Cyril of Alexandria (c.370–444). Despite his strong insistence that Christ is one person, Cyril was no Monophysite, and his commitment to maintaining the reality of Christ's humanity is beyond doubt. In a work written prior to the controversy with Nestorius he wrote: 'He (the Word of God) has not refused to descend to such a low position as to bear all that belongs to our nature, included in which is ignorance.'[11]

In this, as so often in this work, the Alexandrian Patriarch was echoing his predecessor, Athanasius. Cyril was clear that the reality of Christ's humanity brings with it the reality of such human characteristics as hunger, fatigue, fear, sadness and dread of death.[12] One might have thought that this principle would have extended to the reality of ignorance also, but in this case the special nature of such spiritual activity leaves Christ's native human ignorance open to being cancelled from within by his divine knowledge. All that remains is the 'right' to act from time to time as if he did not know.[13] The following statement, from the same work quoted in the preceding paragraph, is unequivocal: 'Christ acts in accordance with the economy of salvation when he says that he does not know the hour, although in reality he does.'[14]

This tension between contrary aspects in Christ received a significant endorsement in Chalcedon's teaching on the two natures in him. However, the enduring influence of Cyril, both in the council and subsequently, ensured that this distinction remained dominated by the sovereign unity of personhood. An interesting sidelight on this council is given us in an anonymous document, *De sectis*, written about a century and a half after the time of which it speaks.[15] Having referred to the problem with regard to Christ's knowledge, the author says that many of the fathers of the council, 'indeed almost all of them', seem to have held ignorance in Christ.[16]

Assuming that this text is a reliable piece of information about Chalcedon, despite the lapse of time involved, one can fit it better into what we know of the council by applying it loosely to more than one line of approach. It applies directly to what we know of the views of the Antiochene minority,[17] but given the kind of statements made by Cyril and Athanasius about ignorance in Christ's humanity, even though they did not quite mean what they seemed to mean, the *De sectis* author may have been including them also in his judgement.[18] Such statements reflect the imperfect state of development of the systematic theology of these authors concerning Christ's knowledge. In the time after Chalcedon, while the doctrine on the distinction of natures eventually bore fruit in a clearer differentiation of divine and human in Christ, it all tended to be qualified, as we have seen, by Cyril's insistence on Christ's unity of personhood. What this meant for the issue that concerns us appears more clearly in the fourth period of patristic development.[19]

*The struggle with Monothelites and Agnoetes*

This final patristic period concerning our topic was part of the theological ferment associated with Monophysitism and Monotheletism.[20] Ever since the conclusion of the Council

of Chalcedon, support for the Monophysite tendencies condemned at that council continued to flourish throughout the
Eastern Church. It was precisely in order to appease these
sympathies that Justinian had summoned the Second
Council of Constantinople (551–553).[21] Even after this gath-
ering the ferment continued, and it was out of this situation
that a movement called Monoenergism, and eventually
Monotheletism, emerged.[22] If agreement could not be found
to express the unity in Christ through there being one
'nature' in him, then perhaps it could be expressed through
the notion of one 'operation' (Greek: *energeia*) or one 'will'
(Greek: *thelèma*) in Christ. This development was particularly significant for our purpose in that it brought into the
centre of discussion some basic principles regarding Christ's
consciousness. These principles received significant support
from the magisterium at this period, and so they remain as
part of the parameters of any discussion of these problems
even today.

For the course of the Monothelite controversy, culminat-
ing in the Lateran Synod of 649 and in the Third
Ecumenical Council of Constantinople in 681, I refer to the
standard histories of theology. The important fruit of these
councils for our subject is the defined teaching on a duality
of wills in Christ. Monoenergism had proved to be a false
dawn, so that eventually people came to see that, to do justice to the depths of the incarnate Lord, two levels of operation had to be acknowledged in Christ, the divine and the
human. The Third Council of Constantinople applied this
principle to Christ's will and freedom. Today we would wish
to extend it to the whole area of his conscious activity.

As well as questions of Christ's freedom, there was some
discussion in this period concerning Christ's knowledge.
The issue was raised in the middle of the sixth century by
a deacon of Alexandria called Themistius, proposing the
thesis that there were some things which Christ simply
did not know. This view was taken up by a number of supporters, who came to be called Agnoetes (Greek: *agnôsis*,
meaning 'lack of knowledge').[23]

Fifty years after the time of Themistius his ideas were still
in circulation, and it was then that the topic became a subject of correspondence between Eulogius, Patriarch of

Alexandria, and Pope St Gregory the Great (590–604). In a letter to Eulogius, Gregory had no doubts that Nestorianism was the hub of the question. In a phrase which should give pause to anyone reflecting on this problem today, he says, 'Unless you are a Nestorian, you cannot be an Agnoete.'[24] Gregory, however, is concerned with Christ's divine knowledge rather than with his exceptional human knowledge. In this connection he gives us a new distinction: Christ has fullness of knowledge existing *in* his humanity but not *from* his humanity. He considers that the latter negation is sufficient basis for the assertion of lack of knowledge in Mark 13:32.

The difficulty we mentioned in the preceding paragraph about extending the duality in Christ into his knowledge in a truly significant way is illustrated by the writings of St Maximus the Confessor (+662), one of the great protagonists of a distinction of wills in Christ. Maximus was strongly opposed to the notion of any human ignorance in Christ. He saw this as tantamount to reducing Christ to a human being and nothing more. We will cite a passage from him which will show how, towards the end of patristic times, the consensus on the absence of ignorance in Christ was being expressed:

> If, then, among the holy prophets, things which were at a distance and beyond the scope of our power were recognized through the power of grace, how much more did the Son of God, and through him his humanity, know all things – not of the nature of that humanity but through its union with the Word? Just as iron in the fire has all the properties of fire, since it both glows and burns, yet in its nature remains iron and not fire, so too the humanity of the Lord, in so far as it was united with the Word, knew all things and displayed attributes proper to God. However, in so far as his human nature is considered as not united to the Word, it is said to be ignorant.[25]

## Examples from the West

Apart from the reference to Ambrose earlier in this chapter, the examples we have cited have all been from the Eastern Church, which was the principal theatre of christological controversy in those times. The matter, however, was also treated by Western writers, of whom we will consider only two, one from before Chalcedon and one from the ensuing period.

The first we turn to is Augustine (354–430), whose ideas are so formative for all subsequent tradition in the West. Unfortunately nowhere does Augustine give us a complete systematic account of Christ's knowledge. His references to the topic come piecemeal, with the result that there remains a certain lack of agreement among his commentators as to his real meaning.

One point, however, is clear and beyond dispute: nowhere does Augustine allow that ignorance should be attributed to the incarnate Word. In his writings this principle stands out clearly, but without the familiar distinction, 'as man' – 'as God'. Even in the one or two places where a form of this distinction is found in the context of knowledge, there is no attribution of ignorance to Christ as man.[26] This fact is all the more striking in that Augustine makes frequent use of this very distinction when he comes to speak of development in Christ. He has no hesitation in accepting the evidence of growth in Luke 2:52 and in predicating it of Christ's humanity. How exactly this perspective is to be combined with the denial of ignorance in Christ is something that Augustine has left obscure.

One of the most far-reaching contributions of Augustine to our topic is his notion that Christ on earth experiences the vision of God. While this notion is not proposed by him with the systematic rigour which characterized the scholastics' approach to the question, it is surprising to find it there in any form, such as we read in the *Contra Maximinum*:

> As regards the statement, 'Not that anyone has seen the Father except the one who is from God; he has seen the Father' (John 6:46), the expression 'anyone' can be referred to human beings (in general). Since the one who was then speaking in the flesh was a human being, his statement is equivalent to his saying, 'Not that anyone sees the Father except myself.' Who is the wise person who will understand these things?[27]

Given the place of Augustine in the theology of the Middle Ages, it is not surprising that these ideas of his are destined to grow in clarity and influence, but, as this chapter has surely made clear, his is no solitary voice. In him we can see coming to expression an exalted understanding of Christ and of his knowledge which was widely shared in the patristic Church.

Augustine died twenty years before the Council of Chalcedon. Over half a century after that council had concluded, the last of the patristic writers we will consider, St Fulgentius of Ruspe (465–533), came on the scene. In him we can see something of how the influence of Chalcedon affected the discussion. The distinction of natures, established emphatically by the council, made it clearer than it had been that the words and actions of Jesus could not be attributed *immediately* to the divinity. In the East, as we have seen, this led to the problem about the reality of Christ's human will. In Fulgentius it enabled the forming of a new question as follows: given that the divinity clearly has an awareness of itself, what kind of awareness of the divinity is present to the human soul of Christ? The sophistication of this question anticipates the subtlety of the Middle Ages, while its interest in *self*-awareness marks a new horizon of enquiry which we associate in particular with our own time.[28]

A fundamental principle for Fulgentius is the distinction in Christ between divine and human knowledge, even when focused on the one object, his own divinity. Unlike the Second Person within the Trinity, his human soul does not have an exhaustive knowledge of the Father. Consequently, the soul's knowledge of Christ's divinity has to be different from that enjoyed by the Eternal Word within the Godhead. At the same time Fulgentius considers it contrary to the faith to imply that Christ's human soul did not have a full awareness of Christ's divinity. In other words, he takes it for granted that there is an immediacy of communication of divine knowledge, not simply to the man Jesus, but to his human knowledge as such. Despite therefore the distinction of natures, we can see even in this case that the unity of personhood is the ultimate determinant of the mind of the God-man.

Together with some other authors in late antiquity, Fulgentius has been taxed with pressing the last principle too far, ending up with attributing to the humanity of Christ the omniscience of the divinity itself.[29] It is true that some passages in him can be read in that confused sense,[30] but in some, if not in all of these patristic writers, the confusion is probably due more to the imperfection of their systematic categories than to a serious Monophysitism. This difficulty only points to the need for a more accurate and systematic reflection on the matter, which it will be the task of the Middle Ages to attempt.

### Conclusion

With Fulgentius we come to the end of our survey of the patristic period on the topic of Christ's knowledge. The evidence we have examined illustrates how the topic arose largely in relation to other christological issues which were the principal areas of concern throughout this period. At the same time, it was an issue never too far from the centre of discussion, and at times it was pursued with vigour and resourcefulness. One of the remarkable features for us in these debates was the way the same texts of scripture, which figure in our discussions today, such as Mark 13:32 and Luke 2:52, were pondered and disputed with no less emphasis then than now. The development of the topic was never straightforward, and it was only towards the end of the period that a real consensus emerged, summed up by Bernard Lonergan as follows: 'From the beginning of the seventh century, both in the East and in the West, the common opinion had it that, even as a human being, Christ was free from ignorance.'[31]

This then was the legacy on Christ's knowledge which the ancient writers bequeathed to their medieval successors. Though, as will appear in the next chapter, the Western medieval development was often original and complex, the force of the patristic consensus was such that, throughout the medieval period, and even up to our own day, it has formed a presupposition in our theology which cannot easily be set aside. However, given the continuing lack of clarity concerning how divine and human come together in the sphere of knowledge and consciousness, one wonders whether one can endow that consensus with the definitive force which authors like Lonergan seem to grant it.

NOTES

1   E.g. Irenaeus, *Against the Heresies* II, 28, 6 (PG 7:808; RJ 204).
2   E.g. Athanasius, *Against the Arians* III, 43 (PG 26:413; RJ 774); cf.
    Gregory of Nazianzen, *Discourse* 30, 15 (PG 36:124; RJ 992). I have
    examined this aspect of Athanasius' viewpoint in more detail in my
    article 'Patristic Approaches to Christ's Knowledge: Part I', *Milltown
    Studies* 37 (1996), pp. 65–81. In that article I continue to assume
    the Athanasian authorship of the Third Discourse against the
    Arians, despite the arguments for an Apollinarian author in
    C. Kannengiesser, *Athanase d'Alexandrie, évêque et écrivain* (Paris:
    Beauchesne, 1983).
3   For instance, *Against the Arians* III, 46 (PG 26:421).
4   To describe this appearance of ignorance, scholars have developed
    the notion of *ignorantia de jure*, e.g. A. Grillmeier, *Christ in Christian
    Tradition* I (London: Mowbray, 1975), p. 315.
5   Gregory of Nazianzen, Letter to Cledonius 101 (PG 37:181; RJ 1018).
6   Gregory of Nazianzen, *Discourse* 30, 15 (PG 36:124; RJ 992).
7   Ambrose, *Treatise Sent to Gratian concerning Faith* II, 11; V, 16
    (PL 16:580; 688f).
8   Ambrose, *On the Mystery of the Lord's Incarnation* 7, 72 (PL 16:837A).
9   Nestorianism was characterized by an insistence on the duality of
    divine and human in Christ to the point that it often seemed not to
    do justice to Christ as one person, one and the same subject of divine
    and human attributes.
10  Examples would be Diodore of Tarsus (*c.*330–*c.*394), *Latin Fragments*
    I, text in *Word and Redeemer*, ed. J. M. Carmody and T. E. Clarke
    (Glen Rock: Paulist Press, 1960), p. 132; Theodore of Mopsuestia
    (*c.*350–428), *Catechetical Homilies*, text *ibid.*, pp. 84–7.
11  Cyril, *Thesaurus on the Holy and Consubstantial Trinity*, 22
    (PG 75:369), as cited by Raymond Brown in his influential book on
    Christ's knowledge, *Jesus God and Man*, p. 102, and repeated in the
    same author's *Introduction to New Testament Christology*, p. 28, n. 28.
12  Cyril, *On the Right Faith* 21 (PG 76:1164AB).
13  This is the meaning of that *ignorantia de jure*, mentioned above note
    4, by which some modern scholars interpret Athanasius and Cyril on
    the appearance of ignorance attributed to Christ in the gospels. See
    Grillmeier, *Christ in Christian Tradition* I, p. 315; II, 2, p. 317.
14  Cyril, *Thesaurus* 22 (PG 75:377D), as translated in Grillmeier, *ibid.*
    II, 2, p. 371. Christ's human knowledge as a spiritual activity is excep-
    tional in the list of the human limitations attributed to Christ. It does
    not seem to me that this is sufficiently allowed for in the discussion
    in J. A. McGuckin, *St. Cyril of Alexandria: The Christological
    Controversy, Its History, Theology and Texts* (Leiden: Brill, 1994),
    pp. 133–4, 216–22.
15  This document, dated at the end of the sixth century, is found among
    the writings of Leontius of Byzantium, but is attributed in the docu-
    ment itself to an otherwise unknown 'Leontius the Scholastic'.
    Scholars now tend to the view that this Leontius is neither Leontius

of Byzantium nor Leontius of Jerusalem: Grillmeier, *Christ* II, 2, pp. 493f (T. Hainthaler). From internal evidence it apears that the author is a strict Chalcedonian.

16 *De sectis* X, 3 (PG 86:1262f). Lebreton remarks that this text 'is the last in Greek patristic literature where an affirmation of human ignorance in Christ is found'. J. Lebreton, *History of the Dogma of the Trinity* (London: Burns, Oates & Washbourne, 1939), vol. 1, p. 428.

17 See references in n. 10 above.

18 About this statement of *De sectis*, Grillmeier makes the cryptic comment that it is 'to be understood against the background of the anti–Arian discussion': Grillmeier, *Christ in Christian Tradition* II, 2, p. 381, n. 270. The rebuttal of Arianism was the point in the distinction 'as man' – 'as God', which was outlined in the account of Athanasius above.

19 Given the leading influence of Athanasius and Cyril in the East, and that of Augustine in the West, it seems to me misleading to imply that the two schools of thought on Christ's knowledge in patristic times, that denying ignorance in him and that conceding it, were of equal strength, as is done in a recent work: B. Sesboüé, *Pédagogie du Christ* (Paris: Cerf, 1994), pp. 142–5.

20 Monophysitism was characterized by its emphasis on the unity of personhood in Christ (expressed through the phrase 'one physis') to the point that it often seemed not to do justice to the reality of Christ's humanity. Monotheletism was the view which would speak of only one will in Christ.

21 In the context of this council the first statement of the magisterium on Christ's knowledge is to be noted. However, it is not a document of the council but of Pope Vigilius in dispute with the council: ND 619/4.

22 The emergence of Monoenergism as a movement is usually associated with the debates of the 630s, but recent research has discovered the central thesis a full century earlier in the writings of Severus of Antioch and Theodosius of Alexandria: Grillmeier, *Christ in Christian Tradition*, II, 2, p. 372.

23 For a recent presentation of this material see Grillmeier, *ibid.* II, 2, pp. 362–82.

24 ND 624–6; DS 474–6. Actually Themistius was no Nestorian but a member of the anti-Julianist wing of the supporters of Severus of Antioch. We might note that his name was included in a list of notorious heretics in canon 18 of the Lateran Synod of 649: DS 519.

25 Maximus the Confessor, *Questions and Doubts*, Answer 66 (PG 90:840). The last phrase in our quotation illustrates how Maximus is in the line of Athanasius and Cyril in making statements about ignorance in Christ's human nature which do not mean what they seem to mean. For an assessment of Maximus see J. Ternus in *Das Konzil von Chalkedon*, ed. A. Grillmeier and H. Bacht (Würzburg: Echterverlag, 1954), vol. III, p. 114.

26 Augustine, *On the Trinity* I, pp. 11–12, 23 (PL 42:836). See T. J. van Bavel, *Recherches sur la christologie de saint Augustin* (Fribourg: Editions Universitaires, 1954), pp. 157–61.

27  Augustine, *Against Maximinus* II, 9 (PL 42:763), translating the final obscure sentence according to the interpretation of van Bavel, *Recherches*, p. 166.

28  Fulgentius, *Letter to Ferrandus*, 26, 31 and 36 (PL 65:416, 420, 422; RJ 2238–39).

29  This criticism has also been levelled against Eulogius, St Maximus the Confessor and St John Damascene: B. Lonergan, *De Verbo incarnato*, ad usum auditorum editio tertia (Rome: Gregorian University, 1964), pp. 356 and 393.

30  For instance, *Letter to Ferrandus*, 29 (PL 65:418–9). Certainly this was the way in which he was understood by some in the early Middle Ages, e.g. Hugh of St Victor, *De sapientia animae Christi* (PL 176, notably col. 845; 848; 851).

31  Lonergan, *De Verbo incarnato*, p. 395. The context of that remark is as follows: 'A special concern of the Fathers, though not the only one, was whether there was anything which Christ as a human being did not know ... Gradually a universal consensus was formed. From the beginning of the seventh century, both in the East and in the West, the common opinion had it that, even as a human being, Christ was free from ignorance ... If we admit that this consensus was formed, to an extent, contrary to the evidence of scripture, we should also say that it was because of scripture that it came about the way it did' (pp. 353 and 395). Translation of the text of this work, here and below, is by the author of this book.

# 5

## ▨ *The Middle Ages*

If the theology of Christ's knowledge in the patristic period came to be dominated by the divinity of Christ, it was left to the Western medieval tradition to work out more clearly how his humanity and his human faculties entered into the picture. This fits in with the general inclination of the times. One of the defining features of the Middle Ages over against the earlier centuries was the way the humanity of Christ received a new emphasis in art, poetry, spirituality and liturgy. However, in the case of the theology of Christ's knowledge, this came about under the shadow of Augustine to such a degree that only to a very limited extent was ground yielded to more empirical approaches, such as those inspired by the philosophy of Aristotle.

Throughout the Middle Ages the fundamental principle under which Christ's knowledge was approached was the universal conviction of theologians concerning the perfection of Christ, 'full of grace and truth' (John 1:14). Keeping in mind the weight of tradition which had built up over the patristic period behind the truth of the Saviour's divinity, this basic principle of the medievals can scarcely be surprising; and this perfection in Christ was extended by them to include his human knowledge. Around the middle of the twelfth century Peter Lombard made it clear that, corresponding to the two natures in Christ, there exist in him both divine knowledge and human knowledge. In the patristic period this point had not always been taken into account in a clear manner, but after Lombard all subsequent theology of Christ's knowledge would be devoted to working out the implications of this distinction.

As remarked already, Augustine was one of the main influences on the entire medieval discussion of Christ's knowledge, and in the light of the explicitly theocentric character of his thought, that is surely not surprising. In particular, his conviction that all our knowledge is a participation in the divine knowledge prediposed medieval theology to the notion that Christ's knowledge is 'from above' rather than 'from below', but in the early thirteenth century the problem was given an unexpected twist when someone applied to it a theorem of Augustine concerning the knowledge of angels, which has come to influence the entire scholastic approach to the question.

Augustine had a theorem about two kinds of knowledge enjoyed by the angels, 'morning knowledge' and 'evening knowledge'. The latter term is his name for the knowledge which the angels have of themselves. Their morning knowledge, on the other hand, arises from their turning to God and to what they discover of the world through knowing God.

In Augustine's case this theorem is never applied to Christ, but that step is taken early in the thirteenth century.[1] Contrary to what one might have expected, this scheme is not seen as a parallel to the Lombard's divine and human knowledge in Christ but as a polarity *within* Christ's human knowledge. Christ's morning knowledge is that by which his human mind knows all things 'in the Word'; his evening knowledge is one drawn from things directly by the experience of the senses. This line of approach had a great appeal for the theologians of the day, and so they applied themselves to developing it and making it more sophisticated. Eventually the evening knowledge of angels was divided into innate knowledge of the world and knowledge of the world drawn directly from experience. In this way Augustine's scheme came to be expanded into a threefold structure, which was commonly applied to Christ as follows:

a. Christ's knowledge of all things in the Word;
b. Christ's knowledge of particular realities through infused ideas;
c. Christ's knowledge of particular realities through the senses.[2]

This threefold model for Christ's human knowing, which had gradually been put together by the work of William of Auvergne, Hugo of St Cher, and particularly by that of Alexander of Hales, came to be accepted by the two great theologians of the thirteenth century, Bonaventure and Aquinas, albeit with certain not insignificant differences between them. Given such an endorsement, one understands better the build-up of authority behind this framework over the subsequent centuries, since it seemed to be the way best guaranteed to do justice to the key points of dogmatic teaching in the matter.

### St Bonaventure (1221–74)

Of the two masters of high scholasticism, Bonaventure remained closer to the Augustinian theology which had lain behind the entire Western tradition of Christ's knowledge up to this point. The basic principle of this approach was both theological and psychological in inspiration: as source of all things, God is not only the ultimate cause of our knowing, but he is so by being also the first object known. In a worldview where this principle was taken for granted, it is easier to see how theologians had so little difficulty in predicating such a fullness of knowledge of the God-man. Bonaventure is no exception, and in him we find clearly accepted a fourfold scheme of knowledge, a modified version of a pattern established in Alexander of Hales:

    a. the Second Person's knowledge in his divine nature;
    b. his human soul's knowledge 'in the Word';
    c. his human soul's 'knowledge of simple understanding';
    d. his knowledge by experience.

Of the first of these we need only recall that this is the knowledge which was the principal issue in the patristic period. In the high Middle Ages the realization was always there that this knowledge is not really distinct from divine personhood, and so must always be kept in mind as an underlying factor whenever we move on to the consideration of Christ's human knowledge.

    Christ's knowledge 'in the Word', namely the beatific

vision, corresponds to that 'morning knowledge' of God we have discussed above.[3] A further question concerns the secondary objects of this beatific vision. The range of Christ's human knowledge, when compared with divine knowledge, had long been a problem in the schools. Peter Lombard had maintained that in his humanity Christ knew as much as the divinity, but not with the same clarity.[4] Such a claim, however, scarcely took account of the necessarily finite nature of any human faculty, even that of the God-man. This was why the often-to-be-repeated formula soon emerged that in his human knowledge Christ knew all actual realities, past, present and future, but not all the unlimited possibles open only to the divine mind.[5]

Bonaventure, however, opened up yet another avenue of approach with a distinction which has remained influential to this day. He differentiates between actual knowledge and habitual knowledge. *Habitually* the soul of Christ knows as much as the Word knows, such is the union between his humanity and the divine Word; but *actually* present to the human mind of Christ from the beatific vision are only such realities as the divine Word wishes to reveal at a particular moment.[6] This distinction between 'actual' and 'habitual' knowledge was one that was taken up by others, most notably by Duns Scotus, and returns frequently in the Franciscan tradition in particular. It is not often realized that Bonaventure himself seems to have moved away from it later and to have adopted a position closer to that which we will find in Aquinas.

Having established his view of Christ's human knowledge 'in the Word' ('morning knowledge'), Bonaventure goes on to the two kinds of knowledge into which 'evening knowledge' had been divided, that by infused ideas, technically called 'species', and that by experience.[7] As regards the former of these two aspects of evening knowledge, according to the general principle of Christ's perfection, if the angels in heaven had innate species, Christ had them also; if the prophets had infused species, so had Christ. Bonaventure called this gift the 'knowledge of simple understanding'. Because of who and what he was and is, Christ on earth enjoyed a plenitude of knowledge second to none.

This also raises a question concerning Christ's experiential knowledge and how it is to be fitted in. In this case Bonaventure makes no significant progress beyond his predecessors. He is aware of the Aristotelian process by which knowledge is derived from the senses, but this is necessary only as a result of the fall of Adam. In the case of the sinless Christ, it cannot be a question of his coming to know something he did not know already, but rather of his now coming to know in a new way, namely by experience, what he already knew in another way by virtue of his higher gifts of knowledge. Nor does Bonaventure allow any reality to the notion of development in Christ. This occurs in appearance only, not in reality.[8] Christ's entering into a fallen world did not require him to take on the defect of ignorance.[9]

## St Thomas Aquinas (1225–74)

When we come to the writings of Aquinas, his position at first seems to be in substantial continuity with his immediate predecessors. The terminology and structure of presentation is much the same. The main lines of knowledge which he attributes to Christ reflect the general fourfold pattern we have already discovered: divine knowledge, beatific vision, infused species and acquired knowledge. But behind the facade of tradition, the inner sources of thought are quite new.[10]

At this stage of its history, theology found itself before a parting of the ways, summed up, perhaps too sharply, by the regent of the Franciscan school at Paris, John Peckham: 'either Augustine or Aristotle'.[11] Up to this time, the influence of the great African theologian, and behind him of Plato, had been all-pervasive in Western thought. However, throughout the twelfth and thirteenth centuries, an alternative philosophy, that of Aristotle, had been gaining ground in the schools. In the work of Aquinas it reached a special highpoint of development.

In the Augustinian–Platonic tradition, God is not only the source and cause of all our knowing, he is its first object. Knowledge in this view was understood as a kind of 'picture-thinking', that is, that we know basically by taking a look at the object known, even if this involves looking at truths inscribed in the divine mind. In Aristotle, on the other hand, the point that makes all the difference lies in taking the forms of things out of the divine mind and seeing them embodied in material reality. This undercuts the primary model of human knowledge as an activity descending from God. In this view the dominant notion of how the mind works has to be of knowledge derived from the senses.

It is clear that, in the Augustinian model, the traditional *a priori* notion of Christ's knowledge is perfectly at home. With the emergence of the Aristotelian model, theology found itself faced with the notion that ordinarily human beings, in their reaction to the world around them, are the agents of their own knowledge. Of course, our Lord was no ordinary human being, and so it was not immediately clear that the inherited tradition concerning his knowledge had to be set aside. A tension, however, had been created between the 'descending' aspects of the traditional view and the *a posteriori* emphasis of the new approach. Aquinas' task, and indeed that of theology generally since that time, has been to try to grapple with this tension.

Against this background we might consider in turn the four main aspects or levels of Christ's knowledge as described by Aquinas. First of all there is his divine knowledge. Since Aquinas is clear that in the Godhead there is no real distinction between person and nature, being and activity, faculty and act, Christ's divine knowledge cannot be really distinct from the divine person. In theology, Aquinas, especially in his later works, is very much a man of the Cyrillan emphasis on the dominance of the divine person; and since he is further convinced that personhood in itself implies a *positive* content of being, then this presence of the divine person and divine knowledge has to mean something actual in him, even though its reality remains beyond our understanding.[12]

When we come to the question of Christ's beatific vision, it is surprising for us to discover that for Aquinas its existence is never in doubt. For him it is simply a datum of faith. As in so many other points of his theology, so here, the emphasis lies less on proving the fact than in showing the appropriateness of what the faith has already established. In this instance the appropriateness arises from the role of Christ's humanity as the instrumental cause of our sanctification and ultimate beatitude. As source and goal of the perfection of the human race, Christ, even as man, has to possess within himself that perfection which it is his mission to bring to the world. As a consequence, if he is to convey a participation in these riches to others, all the treasures of wisdom and knowledge, all the plenitude of grace and beatitude, have to be present in him in a pre-eminent way, indeed as his very own.[13] It is really only within such a heavily theological view of Christ's person and mission that one can find a place for the traditional theses on Christ's knowledge within an Aristotelian approach to the human mind.

The thesis of Christ's beatific vision 'from the first moment of his conception'[14] is the counterpart within his human knowledge of that divine knowledge of the Father which is part of the life of the Trinity.[15] The primary object of the beatific vision is therefore the divine essence. We might notice here in passing how Aquinas takes over from tradition the phrase about knowing 'in the Word'. This relationship to the Word does not mean that the other divine persons are not known as well. The Word is singled out, not as a sole object of knowledge, but as having a particular role in the process of intra-trinitarian knowledge. Within the Trinity the Second Person is the *expression* of what the Trinity is. 'The whole Trinity is expressed by the Word,' says Aquinas;[16] and the union with the Word, which the beatific vision gives to Christ, is a union with the light in which the whole divine essence is seen and expressed by the Word.[17]

Created realities also can come within the scope of this vision in so far as they are present to God; in grasping the divine essence one can grasp these secondary realities also. The question of the secondary objects of the beatific vision has always been problematical for the theologian, particularly when one describes them, as does Aquinas, as embracing all actual realities, past, present and to come. To approach this thesis with some sympathy it is necessary to appreciate that there are two different ways of interpreting such knowledge.

On first hearing this thesis one easily assumes that, according to Aquinas, all these realities of past, present and future are understood to be spread out before the mind of Christ like objects in a landscape.[18] Certainly that is a notion of the thesis held by many scholastics, and it may be assumed to be not far absent wherever the mind is understood to work according to the model of 'picture-thinking' which was ascribed above to the Platonic tradition. Aquinas, however, follows a different model of human knowing based on a notion of how normally the mind disengages the forms of knowledge from the images of reality presented to it by the senses.

According to the 'picture-thinking' approach, concepts are formed as replicas of external reality, and understanding them is a process of considering the various aspects of external reality mirrored in the concept. According to the Aristotelian–Thomistic notion, the process cannot really be described in such imaginative categories at all. It is of a higher order altogether, the way multiple aspects of a reality are grasped as an interrelated unity. One might think of the difference between the free-hand drawing of a circle on a page and the idea of a circle in the mind; the one can be ragged and imperfect, the other is a flawless unity of a circumference in perfect relationship to its radii.

On this latter model the beatific vision is more easily presented, not as a mirror image of another world, but as a grasp of the divine essence and of all in the divine essence which has reference to the beholder, all perceived in one global act, the way multiple realities, like circumference and radii, are grasped in their unity by an act of understanding.[19] The majority tradition of scholastics, such as we find in Bonaventure, tended to follow the 'picture-thinking' model, but Aquinas really broke new ground with the second model. This explains why he did not need the act–habit distinction of the Franciscan school in his account of the vision, and it also explains why his view of this vision leaves more room for a different, more detailed kind of knowledge of these secondary objects through infused species and acquired species.

One of the main difficulties brought up today against the very idea of Christ's vision of God while on earth is the apparent incompatibility between such a vision and the reality of Christ's passion. Behind such a view can lie an assumption that the immediate vison of God has to be as absolute as the divine essence itself. This was not Aquinas.

His reply to the difficulty is to appeal to a special divine dispensation which prevented the joy of the vision overflowing on Christ's lower powers, so that, in the course of his life on earth, his humanity remained subject to all his natural reactions.[20]

This reply has particular significance for our topic: it illustrates how in Aquinas the principle of perfection as the basis of Christ's special knowledge was not proposed in an abstract essentialist way but was open to being qualified existentially by the demands of Christ's mission.[21] Many of those who argue that the reality of the passion rules out Christ's vision of God while on earth are operating out of a maximalist account of that vision which was far from being that of Aquinas. We might add that, once the principle of mission is accepted in this way, then Aquinas' approach is capable of being developed even further, for instance in relation to the problem just discussed of the range of the secondary objects of the vision.

Another aspect of the classical thesis which creates difficulties today arises from the contemporary concern to attribute faith to Christ. Here Aquinas is often taken as the paradigm of those who would deny such a possibility, but in fact his position is not as straightforward as is commonly alleged. It is true that the presence of the beatific vision is held to rule out any basis for attributing faith to Christ, taking these terms in their strict sense.[22] But Aquinas' notion of faith is no rigid conceptualist one. He is well aware of the personalist and affective aspects of the notion, and in one place he could describe faith as the marriage bond between the soul and God.[23] For a purely intellectualist notion of faith there is little room within Aquinas' idea of the beatific vision, but once one brings out the role of the will, of confidence and of obedience, then one can appreciate a remark of his that whatever faith has of perfection may be found in Christ, though whatever it implies of imperfection is excluded in his case.[24]

The third kind of knowledge attributed to Jesus by Aquinas is that through infused species. For many theologians today this is the most questionable aspect of his position, one frequently set aside by people who otherwise count themselves part of the Thomist tradition. The difficulty with it is one already discussed by Aquinas himself, namely that it seems superfluous beside the other kinds of higher knowledge attributed to Jesus.[25] On the other hand, as a form of the special gifts commonly attributed to prophets, it is an aspect of Jesus' supernatural knowledge for which there is some direct evidence in the New Testament.[26]

In the world of Aquinas, the hypothesis of infused knowledge in Christ was so much a part of the tradition that the fact of such a knowledge was not considered a problem. However, in our world, the acceptance of the hypothesis might be said to stand or fall with how one understands Aquinas' answer to the objection of superfluousness. If one focuses one's approach exclusively on the object of knowledge, then indeed is it difficult to make sense of two compartments of knowledge within the one mind, each impervious to the other; but in Aquinas the answer rests rather on the process of knowledge than on its object. The essence of his answer is his insistence that the beatific vision is so out of proportion to our ordinary faculties of knowledge, imagination and expression that in no way does it cut across the usual activities of these powers. This is brought out by a point implicit in Aquinas' notion of the beatific vision but easily missed by modern interpreters of his position. Unlike divine knowledge and the beatific vision, knowledge through species, whether acquired or infused, is the only knowledge proportioned to the discursive nature of the human mind.[27] In themselves, divine knowledge and that of the beatific vision are ineffable and incommunicable. Only when joined to that through species can the revelation imparted through these higher forms of knowledge be translated into communicable ideas and human speech. In this approach, then, knowledge through infused species is essential to the prophetic-revelatory mission entrusted to Christ in the New Testament.[28]

Aquinas' account of the fourth level of knowledge attributed to Christ, namely acquired knowledge, is where we see most clearly the impact of Aristotelian philosophy on the whole subject-matter. In his early writings Aquinas had gone along with the standard approach to the question, which was basically one that denied any role to acquired knowledge in Christ. But by the time Aquinas wrote the *Summa Theologica* he had, as he tells us himself, come to set aside his previous view. In the earlier writings all the 'species' or ideas, which are the units which trigger all knowledge, were seen as derived from the fund of infused species with which Christ was endowed by God. In the *Summa Theologica* he realizes that the intellect God has given to Christ's humanity cannot lie unused and otiose; it must have its appropriate activity, and so a place must be given in our account of Christ for that activity by which we all derive our ideas, the 'species' of understanding, from the imagination and the senses. In this way Aquinas has an answer for the age-old difficulty about progress in Christ's knowledge, and so a basis is laid for the historicity of his humanity which the spirituality and art of the time had already taken to heart.[29]

A case in point is the question of whether Christ could ever learn from another human being while on earth. It is often brought up as a difficulty against Aquinas that he seems to deny the possibility of this in a rather unnuanced way at one place.[30] This, however, can be interpreted as a statement about the basic position of Christ as Revealer of God's truth. It is not intended as an absolute in the way often assumed. Aquinas himself makes this clear when he points out that nothing should be attributed to Christ which is not appropriate to his years; to attribute the perfection of wisdom to the child, he tells us, would reduce the mystery to phantasy.[31] In other words, there is nothing unacceptable in the notion of the child Jesus being taught things by Mary and Joseph.

To us this notion of Christ's acquired knowledge might seem obvious, but in the world of the thirteenth century, still largely dominated by Augustine, it seemed like a revolution. This helps explain why, in some respects, Aquinas did not apply his own discovery as rigorously as he might; nor did he succeed in freeing himself from the maximalist kind of language in which the tradition had come to speak of Christ's knowledge.[32] It is not, however, by such survivals that Aquinas should be judged, but by the originality with which he challenged the established consensus, and by the sense of the reality of the human which he endeavoured to build into his image of Christ.

*John Duns Scotus (c.1264–1308)*

The third medieval theologian we will consider is the famous Scottish Franciscan, who has been called the Subtle Doctor. In some ways he is the most influential of the three figures we have picked out. It is a sign of just how revolutionary Aquinas was that in the subsequent years of the thirteenth century practically no one followed him in his theology of Christ's knowledge.[33] Scotus, however, has had a wide influence, even outside the circle of those who formally number themselves within his school, and this situation has continued right up to our own day. When historians and non-scholastic philosophers speak of 'scholasticism', it is often Scotism they have in mind.

As regards the question of Christ's knowledge, Scotus is firmly in the Augustinian–Franciscan tradition, following on scholars like Alexander of Hales and Bonaventure. For him the first object of all knowledge is God, from whom all the various forms of knowledge descend. Something corresponding to the traditional framework of four levels of knowledge in Christ can be found in Scotus, though he understands the relationship between the levels in his own way. By the beatific vision, Christ in principle can see all that the Word sees, but in practice this is impossible, since this would require a 'perfect attentiveness', which is beyond the capacity of any finite faculty. Consequently, Scotus has recourse to Bonaventure's distinction between habitual and actual knowledge, so that the actual range of secondary objects of Christ's beatific vision is limited.[34] What these in fact are, and how they come before the human mind of Christ, is a matter of divine choice and initiative. Scotus here employs a notion from the Franciscan tradition that the Word of God, as grasped in the vision, constitutes a 'voluntary mirror' (*speculum voluntarium*) in which the objects of the vision are reflected as and when the Word wills.

Knowledge of particular objects for Scotus comes about, not by the abstraction of ideas or 'species', but by adding to such knowledge an intuition of existence. He rejects Aquinas' distinction of knowledge by infused and acquired species as constituting a superfluous doubling of knowledge of the same objects,[35] but interprets Christ's infused knowledge as an abstract grasp of universals, while 'acquired knowledge' is constituted by his intuitive grasp of the existence of particular realities.

By this last theorem Scotus gives his explanation of our Lord's progress in wisdom as mentioned in Luke's Gospel,[36] and some have claimed that in general he gives a clearer account of the historicity of Christ's earthly knowledge than is found in Aquinas.[37] An ontological explanation of this contrast is suggested by Louis Bouyer when he points out that Scotus' general concept of personhood, which he defines in a negative way as the negation of dependence, means that the positive significance of the divine person in the unfolding of Christ's incarnate existence is thereby diminished.[38]

*Conclusion*

Though the preceding pages have given some idea of the diversity and subtlety with which the question of Christ's knowledge was discussed by the medieval theologians, the most remarkable feature of the entire period was the consensus that was continuously maintained regarding the plenitude of knowledge to be found in the God-man. In this way the medieval schools are essentially in continuity with the patristic centuries in which what Lonergan called 'the Catholic mind' was formed to exclude ignorance from Christ. Here we might recall the remark which the same Lonergan included in his survey of the ancient writers: 'We are saying further that the primary cause of this Catholic mind was a very special providence by which, in this as in so many matters, God led his Church forward to the point which he had foreseen and desired it should reach.'[39] While many might be slow today to confess such a confidence in divine providence, Lonergan's belief would have been shared by the medieval theologians and helps to explain why they remained so close to their patristic forbears, thereby strengthening enormously the force of that consensus, which they then passed on to the modern Church with a weight that cannot easily be set aside.

At the same time this chapter will have underlined the diversity in the medieval schools, and in particular the rather fortuitous way in which positions, which later became sacrosanct, were originally put together. This observation seems immediately relevant to the question of infused species, with its curious origin in a theorem about angelic knowledge, but in fact the remark touches on the whole dominance of the Augustinian model of knowledge, which was as widely taken for granted in the Middle Ages as it is widely rejected today.

Our story of the emergence of an Aristotelian account of Christ's knowledge is especially significant. The more empirical approach which it implied, the kind of thing which is so taken for granted nowadays, ran so clearly counter to the tendencies of its time that, on this question, as we have seen, for a generation or two, St Thomas had practically no follower. Indeed it has been suggested by more than one scholar that Thomas himself did not succeed in completely integrating his notion of the human learning process with the tradition on Christ's knowledge.[40] For reasons such as these it can be argued that, despite the at first seemingly unassailable strength of the tradition on Christ's knowledge, the discussion was far from over at the end of the medieval period, with the result that many of these questions have been re-opened in our own time.

NOTES

1  This is probably the work of the Dominican, Hugo of St Cher, writing around 1230, but it is possible that Alexander of Hales anticipated him.

2  Individual theologians sometimes divided Christ's human knowledge in a more elaborate way, but usually containing something corresponding to each of these three kinds of knowledge.

3  Bonaventure here combines under one heading two forms of knowledge distinguished by Alexander of Hales: a knowledge of the secrets of the incarnation and a knowledge of all that belongs to beatitude: J. T. Ernst, *Die Lehre der lochmittelalterlichen Theologen von der volkommenen Erkenntnis Christi: Ein Versuch zur Auslegung der klassischen Dreiteilung: Visio Beata, Scientia Infusa und Scientia Acquisita* (Freiburg–Basle–Vienna: Herder, 1971), p. 114.

4  Peter Lombard, *Sententiae* Liber III, d. 13, n. 8; Ernst, *ibid.*, pp. 91f.

5  Already thus Gandulf of Bologna, *Sententiarum Liber Quatuor*, ed. J. de Walter (Breslau, 1924), p. 348, cited Ernst, *ibid.*, p. 93, n. 15.

6  Bonaventure, *In tertium librum sententiarum*, d. 14, a. 2, qq. 2–3 (Paris: Vivès, 1865), pp. 310ff. It is a special mark of the Franciscan school to emphasize God's freedom in determining how much is to be revealed at a particular moment. As object of the beatific vision, the Word is a 'voluntary mirror' (*speculum voluntarium*) of that which is

to be revealed.

7 Bonaventure, III, d. 14, a. 3, q. 1 (Vivès, p. 319); Ernst, *Die Lehre*, p. 152, n. 30.

8 Bonaventure, III, d. 14, a. 3, q. 2 (Vivès, p. 323).

9 In the background here we can sense an idea which recurs every so often, in the Platonic tradition in particular, by which guilt is interpreted as a function of ignorance. Though the presence of this idea in the patristic writers has sometimes been exaggerated, for instance in St Augustine, it can occur there in varying degrees of clarity. See Grillmeier, *Christ in Christian Tradition* II, 2, p. 364.

10 On Aquinas' approach to Christ's knowledge, see J. P. Torrell, 'S. Thomas d'Aquin et la science du Christ: Une relecture des questions 9–12 de la "Tertia pars" de la Somme de Théologie' in *Saint Thomas au XXe siècle: Actes du colloque du centenaire de la 'Revue Thomiste'* 25–28 *mars* 1993 – *Toulouse*, ed. Serge-Thomas Bonino (Paris: Editions Saint Paul, 1994), pp. 394–409; E.-H. Wéber, *Le Christ selon Saint Thomas d'Aquin* (Paris: Desclée, 1988), especially pp. 199–239; F. Crowe, 'Eschaton and worldly mission in the mind and heart of Jesus' in *The Eschaton: A Community of Love*, ed. J. Papin (Vilanova, PA: Vilanova University Press, 1971), pp. 105–44; G. Mansini, 'Understanding St. Thomas on Christ's immediate knowledge of God', *The Thomist* 59 (1995), pp. 91–124.

11 E.-H. Wéber, *Dialogues et dissensions entre Saint Bonaventure et Saint Thomas d'Aquin à Paris (1252–1273)* (Paris: Vrin, 1974), p. 459. Wéber points out that Thomas can still make use of the Platonic tradition, in particular the writings of Pseudo-Denys, *ibid.*, pp. 184–5.

12 On the question of the formal constituent of personhood in the Thomist tradition, one might consult the standard manuals, such as Lonergan, *De Verbo incarnato*, pp. 222–37.

13 ST III, q. 9, a. 2. Those who, like Karl Rahner, attribute to Aquinas the notion that Christ's beatific vision follows by metaphysical necessity from the Hypostatic Union are criticized by Mansini, 'Understanding St. Thomas', pp. 93–8.

14 ST III, q. 34, a. 4; q. 11, a. 5, obj. 1.

15 Aquinas proposes a parallel between the three forms of human knowledge in Christ and the divine, angelic and human modes of operation: ST III, q. 9, a. 4.

16 ST I, q. 34, a. 1, obj. 3.

17 ST III, q. 10, a. 4.

18 On this see Crowe, 'Eschaton and worldly mission', pp. 113–18, especially pp. 113–14.

19 ST III, q. 10, a. 2.

20 ST III, q. 14, a. 1, obj. 2; q. 15, a. 5, obj. 3; q. 45, a. 2; q. 46, a. 8. Aquinas distinguishes the vision in itself from its consequences, of which the felicity bestowed by the vision of God is one. Such a distinction is less easily made by voluntarists, for whom the essence of the vision and of its felicity lies in the delectation of the will in its object; for Aquinas it lies in the union of the understanding with its supreme end, God: Wéber, *Le Christ*, pp. 219–20.

21  For a different interpretation of Aquinas on this point, attributing to him a more static view of human perfection, see Sesboüé, *Jésus-Christ*, pp. 186–7, citing the view of Maurice Nédoncelle.

22  ST III, q. 7, a. 3.

23  Aquinas, *Exposition of the Apostles' Creed* 1, citing Hos 2:20: *Opera Omnia* (Paris: Vivès, 1875), vol. XXVII, p. 203.

24  *De veritate*, q. 29, a. 4, obj. 15; ST III, q. 7, a. 9, obj. 1.

25  ST III, q. 9, a. 3, objs 1, 2 and 3.

26  The origin of the notion of this kind of knowledge will be found in William of Auxerre's account of one aspect of the 'evening knowledge' of angels, namely of an angelic knowledge of things through the angelic self as an image of God, 'cognitio rerum in seipso', Ernst, *Die Lehre*, p. 100. On the extension of this kind of knowledge from angels to Christ, see n. 1 above.

27  ST III, q. 9, a. 3, obj. 3; q. 11, a. 6.

28  Torrell, 'S. Thomas d'Aquin', pp. 395–7; Wéber, *Le Christ*, pp. 223–4; cf. ST III, q. 9, a. 1, obj. 1.

29  H. Riedlinger points out how Aquinas' use of the gospels in the discussion of Christ's knowledge is more open to the Synoptics than, for instance, Bonaventure, who tends to rely on the Fourth Gospel: *Geschichtlichkeit und Vollendung des Wissens Christi* (Collection 'Quaestiones Disputatae' no. 32; Freiburg–Basle–Vienna: Herder, 1966), p. 89, n. 94; p. 93, n. 107.

30  ST III, q. 12, a. 3.

31  ST III, q. 12, a. 3, obj. 3. For the danger of a 'mysterium phantasticum', see *Compendium theologiae*, chap. 224, St Thomas, *Opera omnia*, vol. 27 (Paris: Vivès, 1875), p. 94.

32  For instance, there is the way he speaks of Christ's acquired knowledge as extending to everything which can be known by the agent intellect: ST III, q. 12, a. 1. Another example is the way he speaks of Christ's childhood: ST III, q. 12, a. 3, obj. 1.

33  Ernst studies twenty-five theologians between the time of Aquinas and the death of Scotus; of these, only one, Johannes Teutonicus OP, follows Aquinas: Ernst, *Die Lehre*, pp. 254, 301.

34  *Opus oxoniense* III, d. 14, q. 2, nn. 20–21 (Vivès edition, XIV, p. 517); Ernst, *Die Lehre*, pp. 270f.

35  *Op. ox.* III, d. 14, q. 3, n. 2 (Vivès, p. 521).

36  *Op. ox.* III, d. 14, q. 3, nn. 7–8 (Vivès, p. 528).

37  Riedlinger, *Geschichtlichkeit und Vollendung*, p. 95, citing L. Seiller, *L'activité humaine du Christ selon Duns Scot* (Paris, 1944), pp. 33–44.

38  L. Bouyer, *The Eternal Son* (Huntingdon: Our Sunday Visitor Inc., 1978), p. 364. On the formal constituent of personhood see Lonergan, *De Verbo incarnato*, pp. 230–35, especially p. 232 on Scotus.

39  Lonergan, *De Verbo incarnato*, p. 395.

40  Crowe, 'Eschaton and worldly mission', p. 114; Torrell, 'S. Thomas d' Aquin', p. 406.

# 6

⊠ *Some Protestant theologians*

The next most significant period in Christology for the purposes of this book begins with the Enlightenment in the seventeenth and eighteenth centuries. In the great upset of the sixteenth century, Christology was not a major issue. The doctrine of Chalcedon remained normative for the Reformers as much as for their adversaries. However, the medieval teaching on Christ's universal knowledge did not escape the criticisms of Erasmus and the Reformers. Luther and Calvin emphasized the aspect of development and the limitations in Christ's knowledge, but it was really only with the turn to human reason as the supreme arbiter of thought, such as marked the eighteenth century in particular, that a significant parting of the ways between Protestant and Catholic scholars became noticeable in the area of Christology.

The publication of the work of Reimarus in 1778 is sometimes regarded as a kind of Enlightenment manifesto against the traditional scholarship of the Bible. Grounded in the Enlightenment rejection of the supernatural, the way was opened for a searching assessment of an 'historical' Jesus shorn of all the privileges of divinity such as the exceptional knowledge which tradition had accorded him. This was not without its benefits for theology, since it helped to bring into focus the humanity of Jesus, to do justice to which remains one of the dominant concerns of all Christology today.

*Friedrich Schleiermacher*

In our necessarily brief survey of the ensuing period, two

developments in particular will be picked out as significant in our story: the response of theology to the Enlightenment and kenotic Christology. Friedrich Schleiermacher (1768–1834) was one of the most original thinkers of the period. His work is a good place in which to see how the Enlightenment insistence on the reality of Christ's humanity enters into a tension with the traditional view of Christ's knowledge and consciousness.

Schleiermacher's Christology could be summed up as a reflection on Hebrews 4:15: 'He was like us in all things but sin.' The German theologian realizes that the exception posed in this text is a very big exception indeed. He gives an impressive account of the sinlessness of Christ, being clear that sin, as a 'disturbance of human nature', takes from our full humanity rather than contributes to it.[1] On this basis Schleiermacher feels he can go on to account for the traditional uniqueness of Christ in so far as his sinlessness has to be rooted in his being. There is much to be said for the judgement of Macquarrie that Schleiermacher did not wish to be reductionist in his Christology but was trying to express in his own terms the essence of what was contained in the traditional creeds and dogmas.[2]

The human person is defined by Schleiermacher as 'a continuing Ego',[3] and it is of interest that Christ's unique consciousness of God is said to be 'implanted in the self-consciousness of the person'.[4] However the way this God-consciousness is implanted in Christ is different from the way it exists in the rest of us. In Christ's case, God is continually and exclusively determining every moment of his existence, whereas in our case the divine influence is adulterated by the activity of our own sensuous self-consciousness.[5] As a result, there is in Christ, and only in him, 'an existence of God in the proper sense'; and 'this perfect indwelling of the Supreme Being' is said to be not only Christ's 'peculiar being and His inmost self',[6] but also 'the innermost fundamental power within him, from which every activity proceeds and which holds every element together'.[7]

The interest of this line of approach is that it is one of the first significant attempts to develop a Christology out of human subjectivity. For this reason Schleiermacher has appropriately been named 'the father of consciousness Christology'.[8] The concern with Christ's sinlessness focuses our attention on Christ's interiority, and this links up with Schleiermacher's characterization of religion generally as 'the highest grade of human self-consciousness'.[9] Piety in this view is the feeling of absolute dependence, and the sense of the *source* of this feeling is what the word 'God' existentially means for us.[10] 'God-consciousness', therefore, is what religion is all about, and the Redeemer's sharing with us the God-consciousness that existed in him is the way his influence enters our lives: 'The Redeemer assumes believers into the power of his God-consciousness, and this is his redemptive activity.'[11]

At this point we must notice that the pre-eminence of this God-consciousness in Jesus is understood by Schleiermacher in moral rather than in cognitive terms. This enables him to face the question of development. While on the one hand Christ's pre-eminence – what Schleiermacher calls 'the ideal' in him – has to be seen as present in him from the beginning of his human existence, yet this is not a presence in fullness but only 'as a germ'.[12] Any suggestion that Christ in his temporal consciousness had a recollection of a separate existence before the incarnation would destroy the reality of his human life.[13] The traditional doctrine of a twofold mind and a twofold will is explicitly rejected.[14] So too the thesis of Christ's omniscience, since this would contradict his true humanity. This sense that the reality of Christ's humanity is incompatible with the late patristic and medieval tradition on Christ's supernatural knowledge remains widespread in Protestant theology to this day.[15]

Another point of interest is Schleiermacher's attempt to describe how finite and infinite come together in every human being, so that Christ can be described as the unique case of something in all of us. True religion, he said, is 'sense and taste for the infinite'.[16] In the author's mind this definition of religion is equivalent to his later one of the 'feeling of absolute dependence', but the former definition is of interest to us as anticipating contemporary language on the transcendentality of human knowledge and freedom reaching out for the divine.

Jesus, for Schleiermacher, is described as 'the completion

of the creation of man',[17] the only one in whom 'the creation of human nature, which up to this point has existed only in a provisional state, was perfected'.[18] Readers of contemporary theology will be reminded at this point of the teaching of people like Karl Rahner: the fact that an incarnation has taken place indicates that there must be in human nature as such a potency, albeit an 'obediential' one, for being assumed into the divine.[19] 'Only someone who forgets that the essence of man is to be unbounded ... can suppose that it is impossible for there to be a man who, precisely by being man in the fullest sense (which we never attain) is God's existence in the world.'[20] Schleiermacher does not hesitate to speak of Christ as 'a human person', being understandably unhappy with the notion of an 'impersonal' human nature, but he is clear that the Person of Christ, right from the very beginning of life, was the outcome of 'the uniting divine activity' which constituted him a unique person and a unique instance of God-consciousness.[21]

From all this it is perhaps clear that Schleiermacher's Christology is very much a Christology from below. As Macquarrie remarks, he started bravely, in the spirit which was to mark nineteenth-century theology, along the road which takes its starting-point from the human Jesus, but the divine aspect of the mystery 'he introduced in a clumsy manner and fails to give an integrated account'.[22] However, the hub of the difficulty in this approach lies not exactly in the passage from the human to the divine but rather in that from consciousness to being, namely to the kind of being which makes the rest possible. After all, as the classical tag has it, activity follows on being.[23]

The central difficulty for any Christology which wishes to begin with consciousness lies in how one is to develop the ontological structure which explains the anomalies and antinomies of Jesus' consciousness, such as they are attested in scripture and tradition. Though Schleiermacher does make a few statements tending in this direction, which have been quoted above, his view that the notion of divine nature is incurably a source of confusion leaves him seriously out of sympathy with classical Christology and with its underlying metaphysics, and this in turn leaves him without the intellectual equipment for negotiating the transition from a 'consciousness' Christology to a Christology of being, such as would be in continuity with the classical tradition of Christianity.[24]

Contemporary with Schleiermacher, though several years his junior, is the even more influential figure of Hegel (1770–1831). Hegel's attempt to marry philosophy with Christianity might at first raise expectations as regards the particular question of this book. However, his theological interest concerned rather the speculative doctrine of the Trinity than the concrete problems of the historical Jesus. Hans Küng has remarked that Hegel had no real positive interest in the text of the Bible beyond three quotations, all three concerned with the Spirit (2 Cor 3:6; John 4:24; John 16:13).[25] At the same time, the impact of Hegel's thought on theologians has been considerable. The work of D. F. Strauss is a case in point, where Hegel's contrast between the speculative order and that of concrete representation was radicalized into the distinction which has so captivated Protestant writers in particular, that between the Jesus of history and the Christ of faith.[26]

Immediately relevant to the problem of this book was Hegel's notion of development. Nietzsche once remarked that without Hegel there would have been no Darwin.[27] In Hegel it is a question of evolution from the less perfect to the more so, rather than an emanation from a perfect Eden to a lesser state. After his time the notion of evolution, both external to Christ and within his consciousness, became a dominant one in Christology.[28]

*Kenotic Christology*

One way in which this notion was implanted lay in the kenotic theories held by several late-nineteenth- and early-twentieth-century writers. This is the second major area of movement in our topic which marked the period from the Enlightenment up to our own day. The notion of *kenosis* or self-emptying as applied to the incarnation owes its origin to the famous hymn incorporated by Paul into his letter to the Philippians (2:5–11). It did not escape the attention of the patristic writers, who generally took as the subject of the self-emptying the pre-existent Word of God. In this way the self-emptying was understood in an extrinsic manner: the emptying of the form, wrote Hilary, is not the abolition of the nature.[29]

The renewed interest in *kenosis* in modern times owes its origin to some christological disputes within Lutheranism already in the sixteenth century, where the issue was not whether the attributes of the divine nature could be predicated of the incarnate Christ, but whether he concealed their use during his earthly life or renounced it altogether. Kenoticism in the strict sense, albeit in varying forms, emerged only in the nineteenth century. It can be defined as the attribution to Christ of a self-limitation of the divine in order to do justice to the reality of his humanity, while at the same time not abandoning the truth of his divinity.

The phrase 'self-limitation' goes back to one of the most famous protagonists of this approach, Gottfried Thomasius (1802–73). Thomasius was a Lutheran, and in the tradition of Evangelical theology, as distinct from the Reformed tradition, he emphasized the unity of personhood in Christ. However, he felt this could not be maintained without some kind of adjustment of the divine to the human in Christ. For this he proposed this notion of the 'self-limitation of the divine'. He distinguished between the immanent and the relative attributes of God. The former he saw as characterizing the relationship of God to the world; examples would be omnipotence, omniscience, omnipresence. The latter he defined as belonging to God independently of his relationship to the world, such as holiness, power, truth and love. In the incarnation the Son would have divested himself of the former but retained the latter.

Thomasius' theory soon ran into considerable criticism from his fellow Lutherans. It was seen to threaten the central doctrine of Christ's divinity and to contradict the concept of divine immutability. The reaction, however, to these criticisms served only to move the discussion from the ontological to the psychological plane, and there the idea of kenoticism has continued to exercise its influence, up to our own day, wherever the fact of Christ's divinity is not felt to require a total actuation of divine consciousness within the reality of the God-man.[30]

The idea also had some impact outside Germany. As well

as a certain following in Russia among writers like Solovyev,
Florensky and Bulgakov,[31] there was also considerable interest in the idea shown in England. The first to do so there was
A. B. Bruce in his 'The Humiliation of Christ', in 1881, but
the most outstanding was the Anglican bishop, Charles Gore
(1853–1932). His *Dissertations on Subjects Connected with the
Incarnation*[32] is still worth reading, not least for its treatment
of the patristic period.

Gore has two major concerns in putting his view forward.
First, he is anxious that justice be done to the full humanity
of Christ; and second, he realizes that the problem of
Christ's consciousness involves one in the question of theological method. He is clear that much of traditional Catholic
theology in this area is a conclusion from premisses established by the councils of the Church. As he interprets
scripture, there is a conflict between scripture and tradition
on the matter, and as a good Anglican he wishes to give the
primacy to the New Testament.[33] At the same time, as a good
bishop, he does not sit lightly to the councils of the Church,
and so he ends up in a position of a certain vagueness, which
will be blamed by some as pusillanimity and praised by
others as modesty.

The phrase of Thomasius that the incarnation involves
a real 'self-limitation' of the Word of God is taken up by
his Anglican follower.[34] By this the latter means 'a real self-
abandonment of the exercise of divine prerogative by the
eternal Son'.[35] Unlike Thomasius, however, he does not
see this abandonment as absolute. It remained 'compatible
with the exercise in another sphere, by the same divine person, of the fulness of divine power'.[36] In this way Gore ended
up attributing, in his own phrase, a kind of 'double life'
to our Lord:[37]

> An old writer said of our Lord that within His
> humanity he 'withdrew from operation both His
> power and His majesty.' To this, as we have seen, we
> must add – His omniscience. But withdrawing these
> from operation within the sphere of the humanity He
> yet *Himself lives under human conditions*. And this
> seems to postulate that the personal life of the Word
> should have been lived as it were from more than one
> centre – that He who knows and does all things in the
> Father and in the universe should (reverently be it

said) have begun to live from a new centre when He
assumed manhood, and under new and restricted
conditions of power and knowledge. Is this conceivable, or is there even any line of thought which tends
in the direction of making it conceivable? Especially
in regard to knowledge, does it mean anything to suggest that He, the same eternal Son, should in one
sphere not know what in another, and that His own
proper sphere, He essentially knows? There are some
considerations which may assist us in this difficulty.[38]

The main consideration which Gore brings forward in
reply to the difficulty lies in the nature of sympathy.
Sympathy, by its very essence, implies a kind of double life:

To sympathize is to put oneself in another's place.
Redemptive sympathy is the act of the greater and
better putting himself at the point of view of the lower
and worse. He must not abandon his own higher
standing-ground if he is to benefit the object of his
compassion; but remaining essentially what he was he
must also find himself in the place of the lower; he
must come to look at things as he looks at them; he
must learn things over again from his point of view ...
May not then the sympathetic entrance of God into
human life have carried with it – not because it was
weak but because it was powerful – something which
can only be imagined or expressed by us as a real 'for-
getting' or abandoning within the human sphere of
His own divine point of view and mode of consciousness?[39]

I delay over Gore's exposition to give an example of a kind
of reflection which keeps recurring every so often. Gore's
own treatment of the problem is of only historical interest
today. His use of scripture is considered too literal and his
theological reasoning has been found lacking in rigour.
However, he does focus on the problem in a way that still
evokes an echo, and his ultimate acknowledgement that we
stand before a mystery is not a point which can be ignored
in the long run.

## Process Thought

In a theological climate where the reality of Christ's humanity is the basic axiom of Christology, and the truth of his

divinity is not always as fully vindicated as it might be, the image of Christ's knowledge and consciousness is generally very far from that plenitude of awareness which predominated in theology throughout the patristic and medieval periods. Among the many movements and trends within contemporary theology, one in particular is worth underlining as giving new life to the specific paradox of kenotic theology, which lay, as we have seen, in attributing a diminished human awareness to Jesus while continuing to give some reality to the truth of his divinity. This more recent development is process theology, and as representative of this trend in Christology one might take the Anglican, Norman Pittenger.[40]

Pittenger's principal work on Christology is *The Word Incarnate*. The basic theme of this book is one with echoes of Schleiermacher and even of Karl Rahner, maintaining as it does that in human nature as such there is a transcendental divine principle at the root of our being in virtue of which we all seek union with God in some sense. It is this movement, which exists in all of us in a diffused way, which comes to be 'focused' in the case of Christ in a supreme way. Jesus represents the highest case of union to which all others point. In explaining this view Pittenger appeals to the notion of divine activity, what he calls 'the divine *nisus* in action in the creation',[41] but the fundamental category behind this presentation is the notion of a God related to this world as proposed by Charles Hartshorne and A. N. Whitehead.[42]

With Hartshorne, Pittenger posits a God who suffers with us in deepest compassion and sympathy.[43] It is clear that such a notion of God greatly reduces the problem of traditional theology with any limitations in Christ's knowledge, for it strikes at the root of the tension between Christ's immutable divinity and his developing, suffering humanity. This is a point which is not spelt out in *The Word Incarnate*. There the author insists on the fully human reality of Jesus' mind and psychology, excluding from him any privileged avenues of human knowledge,[44] but in that book he bases this view on the point that Jesus' human nature was individuated in a true human self, a real personality other than that of the eternal Word.[45]

The connection with process thought is more explicit in

the later writings, where Pittenger declares his preference for an 'event Christology' over a 'person Christology'.[46] He cites with approval a phrase of Whitehead, 'A thing is what it does',[47] and so we are not surprised to read in another work: 'Jesus Christ *is* what he *does*. What classical or traditional formulations have spoken of as the natures of Christ are nothing other than the activities which are operative in that event.'[48] The aspect of process is captured in the following statement: 'No man has a nature ... it is a becoming ... and as a becoming it is what a man's selfhood is.'[49] With such an emphasis in ontology, it is easy to see how the problem of Christ's inner awareness is greatly reduced. In such an approach a developmental view of his knowledge and consciousness is only to be expected. Error, also, fits in as a natural part of the process, and Pittenger, in fact, describes the mental activity of Christ as subject to error.[50]

The issue with process theology is ultimately metaphysical, and on metaphysical grounds alone this theology will be unacceptable to many.[51] As regards Pittenger it must be said that the problems he raises with regard to Christ's mind and psychology reach beyond the horizon of his particular philosophy and will have to be answered from a wider perspective.[52] Pittenger, however, is treated here more as pointing to a factor which has an influence in current Christology greater than the group of those with an explicit allegiance to process thought. Inevitably the notion of a caring, suffering God enters more understandably into the parameters of a developing human nature, so that a theologian of this approach will have less difficulty than most in holding that ultimately, as Pittenger puts it, it is precisely the God in Jesus Christ who experiences 'what it is to be a man'.[53]

That concludes our brief survey of some significant Protestant theologians on the question of Christ's knowledge. Given the limits of this book, the choice of authors has had to be selective, and doubtless the choice made will scarcely satisfy every reader. The purpose in mind has been less to list the best-known names than to pick out those whose work highlights basic *theological* issues in the whole subject-matter, issues which tend to recur in one form or another over a wide field; and as will be clear eventually, those issues arise in Catholic as well as in Protestant authors. A secondary purpose has been to indicate something of the history of the topic between the medieval and the modern periods without trying to be complete. In that time most of the movement in the area was on the Protestant side, so that was a further reason for turning to these Protestant writers; it also helps to set the scene for the Catholic theologians in the next chapter, since many of the problems they grappled with, especially in the exegetical field, had been pioneered by Protestant scholars, both those mentioned and others.

NOTES

1 F. Schleiermacher, *The Christian Faith* (Edinburgh: T. & T. Clark, 1960), p. 385.
2 J. Macquarrie, *Jesus Christ in Modern Thought* (London: SCM Press; Philadelphia: Trinity Press International, 1990), p. 208.
3 Schleiermacher, *The Christian Faith*, p. 393.
4 *Ibid.*, p. 386.
5 *Ibid.*, p. 387.
6 *Ibid.*, p. 388.
7 *Ibid.*, p. 397.
8 G. Vass, *A Pattern of Christian Doctrines* (London: Sheed & Ward, 1996), p. 193, n. 78.
9 Schleiermacher, *The Christian Faith*, p. 18.
10 *Ibid.*, p. 16.
11 *Ibid.*, p. 425.
12 *Ibid.*, pp. 381f.
13 *Ibid.*, p. 422.
14 *Ibid.*, p. 394.
15 *Ibid.*, pp. 382 and 411f. For similar remarks in modern writers, see Macquarrie, *Jesus Christ*, p. 354; also W. Pannenberg, *Jesus God and Man* (London: SCM Press, 1976), p. 333, n. 24.
16 F. Schleiermacher, *On Religion: Speeches to its Cultural Despisers* (New York: Harper and Row, 1958), cited in Macquarrie, *Jesus Christ*, p. 197.
17 Schleiermacher, *The Christian Faith*, p. 367.
18 *Ibid.*, p. 374.
19 K. Rahner, *Foundations*, pp. 215–19. An obediential potency is one which can be reduced to act only by being subject ('obedient') to a special intervention of God: *ibid.*, p. 218.
20 Rahner, TI 1 (1961), p. 184.
21 Schleiermacher, *The Christian Faith*, p. 402. On this page

Schleiermacher distances himself from the notion of *anhypostasia* which Protestant scholasticism had developed in the mistaken assumption that it represented classical orthodoxy. The meaning of the term will be explained when this issue returns at the beginning of Chapter 8 below.

22 Macquarrie, *Jesus Christ*, p. 208.

23 'Agere sequitur esse.'

24 Schleiermacher, *The Christian Faith*, p. 410.

25 H. Küng, *Incarnation de Dieu: introduction à la pensée théologique de Hegel comme prolegomènes à une christologie future* (Paris: Desclée, 1973), p. 530.

26 McGuckin, *St. Cyril*, p. 190, draws attention to Nestorian tendencies which can easily lie behind this distinction. On Strauss developing the legacy of Hegel, see Macquarrie, *Jesus Christ*, pp. 224–30.

27 Küng, *Incarnation de Dieu*, p. 19.

28 *Ibid.*, p. 591.

29 St Hilary of Poitiers, *On the Trinity* 9:14 (PL 10:293; RJ 874). Grillmeier points out that *kenosis* is defined in the Pauline text as a 'taking' (Greek: *labôn*, Phil 2:7) – Grillmeier, *Christ in Christian Tradition*, vol. I, p. 21.

30 For instance, J. C. O'Neill, who speaks of the Son of God surrendering for a time his omniscience, *Who Did Jesus Think He Was?*, p. 116, n. 5.

31 On these see F. C. Copleston, *Russian Religious Philosophy: Selected Aspects* (Notre Dame Ind.: Notre Dame University Press, 1988); also B. Schultze, 'Chalkedon in der russischen Theologie' in *Das Konzil von Chalkedon*, edited by Grillmeier and Bacht, vol. III, pp. 719–63, at pp. 736–43, 746–51.

32 Charles Gore, *Dissertations on Subjects Connected with the Incarnation* (London: John Murray, 1907). This book is referred to below as *Dissertations*.

33 Gore, *Dissertations*, p. 205.

34 *Ibid.*, p. 204.

35 *Ibid.*, p. 205.

36 *Ibid.*, p. 207.

37 *Ibid.*, p. 218.

38 *Ibid.*, p. 215, italics in the original.

39 *Ibid.*, pp. 218–19.

40 W. N. Pittenger, *Christ and Christian Faith* (New York: Round Table Press, 1941); *The Word Incarnate* (London: James Nisbet, 1959); *Christology Reconsidered* (London: SCM Press, 1970); *Catholic Faith in a Process Perspective* (New York: Orbis, 1981).

41 Pittenger, *The Word Incarnate*, p. 242.

42 N. Pittenger, *Process Thought and Christian Faith* (New York: Macmillan, 1968), especially pp. 65–74. For process theology in

another author, who later in this book will be compared with Pittenger, see P. Schoonenberg, 'Process or history in God', *Louvain Studies* 4 (1973) pp. 303–19; also *The Christ* (London–Sydney: Sheed & Ward, 1972), p. 85n. More recently process theology has been applied to these problems by G. Vass, in the work cited in n. 8 above.

43 Pittenger, *The Word Incarnate*, p. 149. This last point might seem to recall the view of Charles Gore, but Pittenger rejects kenoticism unequivocally. Referring to the distinction between immanent and relative attributes, Pittenger wrote that the advocates of kenoticism 'create a new set of problems about the being of God himself which are actually more serious than those they have sought to solve', *The Word Incarnate*, p. 110.

44 Pittenger, *The Word Incarnate*, p. 116.

45 *Ibid.*, p. 115. In other words, Pittenger rejects the doctrine of 'anhypostatic manhood', *ibid.*, pp. 102f. As will be discussed in Chapter 8 of this book, Pittenger at this point is close to the views of Piet Schoonenberg.

46 Pittenger, *Christology Reconsidered*, p. 56. This terminology is borrowed by Pittenger from J. Knox, *The Humanity and Divinity of Christ* (Cambridge: Cambridge University Press, 1967).

47 A. N. Whitehead, *Adventures of Ideas* (New York: Macmillan, 1933), p. 161. The phrase is cited and discussed in Pittenger, *Catholic Faith in a Process Perspective*, pp. 23–32.

48 Pittenger, *Christology Reconsidered*, p. 96, his italics. Anticipating this in an early book on the topic, he wrote as follows: 'The deity of Jesus ... is that which is *act of God* in him, that which is act of God through him; or, better expressed, it is God acting through him', *Christ and Christian Faith*, p. 45.

49 Pittenger, *Christology Reconsidered*, pp. 56f.

50 *Ibid.*, pp. 35–9.

51 This issue is more than can be treated here. See D. Burrell, 'Does process theology rest on a mistake?' *Theological Studies* 43 (1982), pp. 123–35.

52 This will be attempted in Chapter 8 below, when Bernard Lonergan's views on Christ's human centre and consciousness will be explained.

53 Thus Pittenger, *The Word Incarnate*, pp. 105f. This position should be related to Pittenger's rejection of the standard doctrine on the interchange of predicates (*communicatio idiomatum*), *ibid.*, pp. 125–6.

# 7

# ⧆ *Some Catholic theologians*

In order to give some idea of how this subject is discussed among Catholics today, rather than presenting the matter thematically, I propose in this chapter to present it from the point of view of three outstanding Catholic theologians, each representative of different perspectives, while agreeing on essentials. These are perhaps the three most influential Catholic figures in the theology of the twentieth century. Other theologians commonly take their bearings from them, so that, in a way, it is the whole field of Catholic theology which is opened up by considering these three figures, even though each of them is no longer among us.

## *Karl Rahner (1904–84)*

The story of our subject in the contemporary period begins with the work of Karl Rahner, since he was the one within Catholic theology whose challenge to the medieval synthesis on the topic has had the greatest impact. With a new starting-point in a more existentialist philosophy, he set out, not so much to deny the prevailing orthodoxy, as to outflank it from an original point of view.[1]

The fundamental Rahnerian principle is the experience of grace offered to every human being in the depths of one's own consciousness. This principle helped to validate the notion of experience, on which much of the truth in modernism was centred. It also gave Rahner his basic analogy for approaching the knowledge and consciousness of Christ. However, at this point Rahner introduces a distinction between reflexive and basic consciousness, and this

distinction is destined to be fundamental to the whole subsequent discussion of the problem. Reflexive consciousness
is the ordinary vehicle of conceptual thought, clear, thematic and propositional. Basic consciousness, while actual, is
pre-conceptual, non-thematic and inarticulate. For Rahner
it is buried in the depths of that awareness of oneself which
is the prior condition of all consciousness and knowledge. In
this way Rahner aligned himself with those who would challenge the identification of thought with concept, which, in
one form or another, had dominated European philosophy
and theology at least since the time of Descartes. This did
not mean that Rahner sat lightly to the concepts and propositions of the tradition of faith – he was no modernist  – but
it did give him a fresh basis from which to work out a new
approach to many truths.[2]

Among these truths were those surrounding the knowledge and consciousness of Christ, and indeed Rahner's
whole Christology is sometimes described as a 'consciousness Christology'.[3] One of the first conclusions from
Rahner's approach was his contention that consciousness is
multi-layered. By this statement he had in mind, in the first
instance, the two levels of consciousness just distinguished.
The point also provided Rahner with a basis for giving new
life to an observation already found in the medieval
theologians, and one that is really central to the entire
debate, namely that a person might know something on one
level while being ignorant of it on another.[4] This realization
was also in line with the findings of another discipline altogether, namely the levels of the conscious and subconscious
as studied in empirical psychology.

Before coming to the heart of Rahner's approach there
are two preliminary points to be clarified. First of all, it
seems advisable to say a little more about what Rahner
means by basic consciousness. By this he refers primarily to
that immediate inarticulate self-presence which is the basic
condition of all consciousness and knowledge. It is not the
knowledge of an object but the condition for the knowledge
of any object. It may be reflected on and described, but
more often than not it is simply passed over and taken for
granted; yet that does not mean that it is not explicitly present in consciousness. Once people are conscious at all, they

have to be conscious of themselves being conscious, and so
the self-presence to which we refer has to be a factor in their
awareness, whether the individual can articulate it in words
or not.[5]

Armed with his distinction between reflexive and basic
consciousness, Rahner was able to take up the question of
Christ's knowledge in a new way. As we have seen already,
the challenge to the traditional scholastic synthesis was coming mainly from contemporary exegesis. Rahner felt that he
could do justice to the central plank of Catholic tradition by
his notion of basic consciousness, while all that the exegetes
were saying could be accommodated within reflexive consciousness. On the level of basic consciousness Rahner
argued that Christ had an immediate consciousness of himself and of his own identity as Son of God. Within this
awareness Rahner located what he referred to as the immediate vision of God.

The second point to be clarified concerns why Rahner
prefers to speak in this way of the *immediate* vision rather
than of the *beatific* vision of God. By this he wishes to bring
out that the vision of God, which tradition attributes to
Christ, did not mean that our Lord on earth was habitually
filled with the happiness proper to the life of heaven.[6] Even
some of the medievals, as we saw in Chapter 5 above, had
already seen this point and, in order to make room for the
reality of Christ's passion, had postulated that in his case
some of the usual consequences of the vision of God would
have been suspended.[7] By separating the idea of the vision
from that of the fullness of beatitude, Rahner focuses his
notion of the former on the aspect of the union it brings
about between the divinity and the soul, a direct union of
consciousness, which Rahner in fact interprets according to
his famous theorem of quasi-formal causality.[8]

We come now to the main point which Rahner makes
about Christ's vision of God, and we will appreciate it best
by seeing it within its setting in his theology generally.
Rahner's theology is nothing if not comprehensive. It takes
in an entire view of the history and destiny of the human
race, which is seen as governed by the grand design
of the divinity to communicate itself to the world.
Christology is central to this plan, since the grace which is

to be communicated to human beings comes about through first being given to Christ in a supreme and exemplary instance. The divinization of the world hinges on the divinization of the humanity of Jesus, whose unique position requires the unique intensity of grace embodied in the Hypostatic Union.

This then is the setting within which Christ's immediate vision of God finds its meaning. According to the plan for the divinization of the world, the immediate vision of God is the goal and fulfilment of every human being; but as Christ is the source and exemplar of this fulfilment, this vision of God is already found in him, even during his life on earth. Here Rahner gives new life to the medieval assumption that, if Christ is to be the source of all human participation in heavenly knowledge and beatitude, then something corresponding to these graces must be found in him in a supreme degree. As he puts it in one place:

> the intrinsic effect of the hypostatic union for the
> assumed humanity of the Logos consists precisely and
> in a real sense *only* in the very thing which is ascribed
> to all men as their goal and their fulfilment, namely,
> the immediate vision of God, which the created
> human soul of Christ enjoys.[9]

In this perspective it is not too much to say that Rahner places Christ's vision of God at the centre of the religious universe. He sees the entire conscious life of Christ coming to its focal point in the Saviour's surrender to the loving incomprehensibility of God. We will appreciate more deeply here the interconnection of truths if we bear in mind an emphasis that the author makes with regard to the vision of God from his earliest publications on the matter. The beatific vision does not entail the elimination of the mystery of God. Even in heaven the incomprehensibility of the Godhead remains; indeed its very mysteriousness is part of the bliss of its being known and loved.[10] This remains true for the *human* knowledge of the divinity by the incarnate Word, whether on earth or in heaven, and so this truth of the immediate vision explains how, as already said, the entire conscious life of Jesus centres on the act of surrender of his human being to the loving incomprehensibility of God. This is the act which he carried out above all in his death, which is described as Jesus' finally sinking into the incomprehensibility of God; and this surrender becomes the matrix and model of the surrender at the heart of the act of faith of every believer.[11]

However, as well as developing in this impressive way the theological context of Christ's vision of God, Rahner must also face the question of its dogmatic basis. He judges that to attempt to ground the thesis in scripture and tradition in the usual way is unlikely to yield reliable results.[12] For him the thesis is already contained within the truth of the Hypostatic Union itself, and so it must rank as a necessary deduction from that truth.[13] As a premise to that deduction he places what he calls the axiom of a Thomistic metaphysics of knowledge, namely the principle that being and consciousness are ultimately the same thing. 'An existent,' he says, 'possesses being to the degree that the existent is "present to itself" and "returns to itself".'[14] Consequently, when the being of the Word assumes the created reality of Jesus' human nature, as the being of the one enters into the constitution of the being and of the consciousness of the other, so does the self-consciousness of the one become a factor in the self-consciousness of the other. Rahner expresses the point sharply: 'A purely ontic *Unio Hypostatica* is metaphysically impossible to conceive.'[15] It is this impact of the divine self-consciousness of the Word on the human self-consciousness of Jesus which is captured in the soul's immediate vision of God.

What then of the secondary objects of the beatific vision? From the premises just laid down, Rahner goes on immediately to describe the kind of 'mirror image' notion of the vision of God which we ourselves excluded on an earlier page.[16] Rahner rightly points out that it is this naive notion of the immediate vision which seems to run counter to the evidence of the New Testament. He himself excludes it from his concept of the vision of God, not for the reason drawn from a certain view of cognitional process, such as was put forward in Chapter 5 above, but because he locates the vision exclusively at the subjective pole of consciousness rather than at its objective pole.[17]

For Rahner our Lord's direct vision of God can be

described as an elevation of that basic self-awareness which is not itself a knowledge of objects but the prior condition of all conscious relationship to objects. In Christ's case this self-awareness is illuminated by the presence of the divinity through the identity of the divinity with the self of the knower. This helps explain why Rahner speaks of the vision in terms of direct presence *to the Logos* by the human soul of Jesus.[18] This aspect of his teaching has been severely criticized, even by those who would wish to be close to him.[19] The mind of Christ in the New Testament is not centred on the Word but on the Father. Though in his later writings Rahner tends to speak of the vision as simply focused on 'God',[20] the basic notion remains, and it throws light on how the author understands the intellectual development of Jesus during his life on earth.

There are two aspects of this development to be noticed. First, given that Jesus' basic awareness of who and what he is is in principle inarticulate and subjective, there is room for the process by which this ultimate condition within him is translated into objective conceptual knowledge. In this process Jesus would be assisted by his growing knowledge of his environment, and inevitably his eventual articulation of his divine identity would be expressed in terms of his own culture and history.[21]

Second, there is the question of the secondary objects of the vision of God, ordinarily conceived as in some sense included in the visionary's grasp of God. In Rahner's account the scope for these is greatly reduced, though not excluded entirely.[22] They are conceded only within unthematic basic consciousness, and that only in reference to Jesus' life and mission.[23] As he also excludes the thesis of Jesus' special infused knowledge, he has, in this way, left more than ample room for the role of acquired knowledge, without any derogation from his view of the immediate vision of God. Jesus did not carry around in his mind an encyclopedia of propositional knowledge, but had to acquire such objective knowledge the way we all acquire it.[24]

Having opened up in this way a place for lack of knowledge in Christ, the question now arises as to whether our Lord could fall into error. As was mentioned in the third chapter of this book, this point arises in particular in regard to Jesus' expectation of the Parousia. The last day will clearly be a mysterious event, and as we saw in that previous chapter on this topic, there is evidence from the gospels that Jesus' predominant inclination lay in disowning the desire of apocalyptic to calculate its date. This notwithstanding, the question can still be raised whether an erroneous prediction of an imminent Parousia, as suggested by Mark 13:30, would contradict our notion of Jesus' knowledge and consciousness.

Rahner's account of this vexed question is far from straightforward. In principle he accepts the possibility that Jesus declared the Parousia would come 'soon', so that, taken in itself, his statement was erroneous. But Rahner realizes that there is a necessary distinction between meaning and expression. He proposes that a statement of imminent Parousia could be a way of expressing one of the central truths of a realized eschatology, namely the truth of the closeness of God, who calls for an unconditional decision in the here and now, independently of whether the Parousia is to come sooner or later. When understood in synthesis with such a perspective, and in conjunction with Jesus' overriding conviction of the incalculable character of the Day of Yahweh, Rahner considers that our Lord's meaning was not an error; and in this way due respect is shown to the teaching of the magisterium on the point.[25]

I have delayed over explaining Rahner's position on the beatific vision because of its far-reaching influence in theology generally. His was the contribution which broke the deadlock between dogmatics and exegesis and set a headline for all further reflection on the point. Indeed it does not seem too much to say that, once theologians are prepared to enter the discussion at all, they take their bearings from Rahner's contribution. Up to the appearance of Rahner's first essay on the point in 1954, the traditional thesis of Christ's threefold human knowledge was considered universal in Catholic theology. Since that time this age-old consensus has crumbled away.

The present situation might be summed up as follows. All contemporary theologians agree on the reality of Christ's ordinary acquired human knowledge, but it is when they come to his special human knowledge that their paths begin to diverge. There are still some, a dwindling number, who remain, in one form or another, with the traditional theses (J. Maritain, B. de Margerie, L. Iammarone, W. G. Most, F. Ocáriz, D. Ols etc.).[26] Then there are many, perhaps the majority, who go along with Rahner's account, at least in a general way (Gutwenger, Kasper, Riedlinger, Sesboüé etc.). A third path is that of those who are content to shelve the hypothesis of beatific or immediate vision and explain Christ's special human knowledge by some version of infused or prophetic knowledge, though some consider that a special intuition of divinity must be included (Bouyer, Duquoc, Galot, Nicholas, O'Collins, Torrell). It is because of the impossiblity of treating all of these views that I elected at the begining of this chapter to concentrate on three leading and contrasting figures in Catholic theology. We will now go on to the other two theologians, but it must be granted that neither has had the impact in this matter that Rahner has achieved.

## *Hans Urs von Balthasar (1905–88)*

No less profound, but somewhat different, is the work of the famous Swiss scholar, Haus Urs von Balthasar. Among Catholic theologians he is characterized by a certain independence, both in his interests and in his positions, and this has enabled him to develop his own approach to Christ's knowledge, while remaining in sympathy with the more existentialist currents of the day.[27]

Balthasar's whole Christology could be described as one centred on consciousness. This arises from his dissatisfaction with the ontological approach to the notion of the person as found since patristic times. This is not, however, the 'consciousness' Christology found in Protestantism, some examples of which have been discussed in an earlier chapter. It is based on a notion of person defined from mission.

To arrive at this point, Balthasar has made a distinction between the individual and the person. For him 'person' means simply the conscious subject. The individual is defined in opposition to the genus or the species; but since such a notion can be applied at all levels of being, it fails to bring out what is specific of the human conscious subject.

Often, however, in patristic and medieval times, the notion of the individual was pressed into service precisely as though it could fulfil that deeper function, and as a result Balthasar remains dissatisfied with the entire traditional theology of the person.[28] To describe the characteristics of the individual conscious subject within the genus or species, we have from within our experience only empirical approximations. The qualitative uniqueness of the subject inevitably escapes such determinations. Balthasar feels this uniqueness can be defined only by God himself, and this arises once God gives to individuals their mission in life. This is what formally constitutes them as persons.

In describing the knowledge and consciousness of Jesus, Balthasar's approach agrees in its general lines with that of Rahner. He regards Jesus on earth as, to some extent, a *comprehensor*, while remaining a *viator*.[29] This is a way of saying that, while there is sense in the notion that Jesus on earth enjoys the immediate vision of God, this does not mean a static knowledge of all things, past, present and to come. More than once Balthasar refers approvingly to Rahner's account of lack of knowledge in Christ.[30] For Balthasar the best approach to the mystery of Jesus' awareness is the formula about being sent on mission, constantly repeated in the gospels. Balthasar is concerned to avoid turning Christ's temporal reality into a supratemporal one, and so turning Jesus of Nazareth into a demi-god by depriving him of the fundamental human act of self-abandonment to that which is greater than ourselves, be it death or God:[31]

> To regard Christ's knowledge as though he carried out his actions in time from some vantage-point of eternity – rather like a chess-player of genius who quickly foresees the whole course of the game, and simply moves his men through a game which for him is already over – would be to do away entirely with his temporality and so with his obedience, his patience, the merit of his redemptive existence; he would no longer be the model of a Christian existence and of Christian faith.[32]

Balthasar differs from Rahner in his emphasis on Christ's consciousness as essentially a relationship to the Father.[33] He is one with Rahner in the key step of locating Christ's awareness of his divinity within his self-consciousness, but he insists that this means a consciousness of mission, and so it includes a direct relationship to the One who sends, the Father.[34] The key to this situation has already been given with the notion of person as defined from mission. Jesus' awareness of his personhood, albeit in an unthematic way, has to be at once his awareness of his mission and of divinity. Mission is the key which ultimately links his being on earth with his being within the Trinity. His being sent by the Father (*missio*) is simply a modality of his inner-trinitarian proceeding from the Father (*processio*).[35]

Sonship, therefore, and the obedience which is its primal expression, are the fundamental themes of Christ's consciousness and knowledge. Through the notion of sonship, that which the Word is at the heart of the Trinity can be transposed into the language of this world. The Son's being within the Godhead is the uninterrupted reception of everything that he is, his very self, from the Father. The response of such a Son has to be that of adoring assent to the Father, which, however, because of the identity of being and activity in the Godhead, has to coincide perfectly with the fundamental receiving that defines him. Through these categories, while Balthasar is clear about the distinction of divine consciousness from human consciousness, he feels no need, as he puts it, 'to agonize over the relation of his human self-consciousness to this divine self-consciousness'.[36] Christ's fundamental intuition as to his identity, if it could be put into words, would be 'I am the one who must accomplish this task'. That task is the one of expressing through his entire being the Fatherhood of God, expressing it through his life and death in and for the world.

With this doctrine on the being of Christ as his premise, Balthasar can go on to give his interpretation of the various words and deeds attributed to Jesus in the New Testament. The theology of mission is the defining aspect throughout, with the Johannine presentation of the theme seen as only the logical development of what is already implied in the Synoptics. The crux of this whole perspective, which marks the transition from a merely human to a more than human awareness, is the sense of the eschatological. In Jesus' awareness of his mission as *universal*, there opens up a chasm between what he himself can achieve within the limits of his mortal life and the historical fulfilment which God envisages for his life-work. The latter is therefore something which only God can bring about, while Jesus' role is to 'let go' and so surrender himself to God in death. However, unlike John the Baptist, Jesus realizes that in some sense this fulfilment is already *in* him. This is what he reveals by his claim to authority over eschatological salvation (Matt 10:32f), and in this we have evidence that he is aware of an element of the divine in his own innermost self-consciousness.[37]

At the same time Balthasar stresses that this intuitive awareness, which he identifies with the immediate vision of God, is limited by the scope of Christ's mission. Indeed Balthasar postulates the possibility of variation even in Jesus' vision of God. Here he appeals to the analogy of Christian mystical experience, with its alternating heights and depths. At times Jesus' field of attention would have been restricted, for obedience's sake, passing, as it were, through a narrow ravine of darkness, as the particular situation demands.[38]

In the light of such a limitation of knowledge, we can understand Balthasar's approach to the gospel texts which are problematic in this area. On the one hand our Lord expects the imminent arrival of the kingdom, which is to change everything; but on the other, he quietly goes about the task of his mission, day by day, conscious that it is heading for death, but leaving all in the Father's hands.[39] Balthasar is open to accepting as genuine the three standard texts which assume that the final coming of the kingdom is temporally close (Mark 9:1; 13:30; Matt 10:23). He also takes in its most obvious sense the statement on ignorance ascribed to Jesus in Mark 13:32. As Balthasar puts it: 'It is impossible to believe that the community would have been able uninhibitedly to attribute ignorance to him if he had not spoken of it himself.'[40] But this does not mean that our Lord was giving in to the apocalyptic concern for dates and times. The crucial truth is that the reign of God is already breaking in within himself; present and future are intimately bound together; the numbering of days and hours is irrelevant. Thus for Balthasar the notion of an interim period between his death and the Parousia cannot be detected in the gospel texts that come from Jesus. Positing phases in this consciousness of his mission is unacceptable.[41]

Balthasar's concession of limitations in Christ's knowledge and consciousness lays the basis for one further thesis of his, of which he has been one of the most influential protagonists in Catholic theology. I refer to the thesis of Christ as model of faith. As we have seen in earlier pages, theology generally, and scholastic theology in particular, have been slow to list faith among the attributes of Christ, since nowhere does the New Testament refer to Christ as a believer. To some extent this question depends on how one understands faith, and on the degree to which one lays emphasis on the more affective and volitional aspects in that concept.[42] If one defines faith as simply assent to revelation as true on the basis of divine authority, such as was the common notion of Catholic theology after Vatican I, then indeed there seems to be little room for Balthasar's thesis. But once one moves to a notion of faith based on that of Vatican II, where the emphasis lies on the surrender of the whole self, mind and heart, to God, then the groundwork has been laid for seeing the question in a new light.

Obedience to the Father, as we have seen, is for Balthasar the fundamental theme of Christ's knowledge and consciousness, but obedience is also the key to Pauline faith (Rom 1:5), so it is not surprising that Balthasar should want to bring the two attitudes into one. His starting-point, however, lies in the Old Testament and in its notion of faith centred on trust and fidelity. For the Jews the attitude of the believer had its model in God himself and in his fidelity to his promises. This enkindled in the true Israelite an answering fidelity to God and the trust that sustains it through all the trials of life. Now according to the whole movement of the Bible, Christ has perfectly fulfilled the disposition on the human side that God has demanded of believers. Jesus is the incarnate 'faithfulness of God' in whom all the promises of the divinity have found their Yes (2 Cor 1:18-20). The source of the Son's power is the way he refers everything he is, does and says to the Father. This is the model for every believer, but Jesus is the only one who possesses this disposition in its fullness and who can impart it to those who entrust themselves to him.

For all those who wish to attribute faith to Christ, the main, and almost the only, scriptural text they can appeal to is Hebrews 12:2, where Christ is presented as 'the author and finisher of faith'. Balthasar too appeals to this text, but, grounding his thesis on the letter to the Hebrews, he must also face up to the difficulty created by this letter's contrast of faith *versus* sight, as in a common translation of Hebrews 11:1, 'the evidence of things unseen'.[43] The difficulty arises in reconciling this contrast with whatever special knowledge we are obliged to attribute to Christ in his role as Revealer. Balthasar grasps the nettle by simply invoking the limitations of Christ's knowledge. During his life on earth our Lord did not know the paths which God was setting before him for the fulfilment of his mission, but he always had the certainty that the Father would bring it to its conclusion.[44]

That is not to say, however, that there is no difference between the way this 'faith' exists in Christ and the way it is found in believers generally – a point which Balthasar feels some leading Protestant writers have failed to appreciate.[45] We only receive our mission as a consequence of our coming to faith; Jesus always has his mission and *is* his mission. This is why he is the living source of all that this mission implies in us, including our faith. In this way Christian faith comes to be described as 'enfolding oneself into Jesus' most interior attitude'.[46]

That such an outstanding theologian as Balthasar, and one whose respect for church tradition is so well known, should propound the thesis of Christ's faith with such force is a measure of how well established this notion has become in contemporary theology.[47] Other writers, of course, present it, each with his or her own nuance, as, for instance, G. O'Collins in a recent book.[48] It is noteworthy that this author only accepts the concept with the proviso, which Balthasar also insists on, that the notion of faith has to be applied analogously as between Christ and Christians. The ontological and psychological uniqueness of Christ remains fundamental to all Christology. As a consequence some can accept the notion of Christ's faith only while insisting on its being used analogously in his case, while others for this very reason still reject the notion altogether.[49]

*Bernard Lonergan* (1904–84)

Contemporary with Rahner and Balthasar, but ploughing a different furrow, the Canadian scholar, Bernard Lonergan, also merits attention. His position within Catholic theology, on this as on other topics, is more distinctive than at first appears. During his years professing Christology in the Gregorian University, Rome, the general lines of his teaching placed him squarely within the Thomist tradition, but in contrast to the other theologians we have mentioned, his early training had been more eclectic, and he had become a convinced Thomist only comparatively late in his development. Like these theologians also, Lonergan had undergone some influence from Joseph Maréchal, and so is sometimes located within the school of transcendental philosophers and theologians. But here again the influence was not a thoroughgoing one, and so Lonergan is not as easily categorized as some have thought.[50]

Lonergan too had to confront the challenge which post-Enlightenment humanism and, to an extent, modern exegesis had raised against traditional theses on Christ's knowledge. Rahner and Balthasar had responded by shifting their ground on some of these theses, in so far as that was compatible with orthodoxy. Others of a more conservative bent simply remained with the tradition they had always known. Lonergan reacted in a rather defiant but original way. He argued that all we know of Christ's knowledge comes by analogy with our own,[51] but since most people misunderstand their own thought-processes, the first thing to be done is to develop a renewed philosophy of knowledge, which Lonergan himself attempted in his weighty volume, *Insight*.[52]

The key to Lonergan's philosophy of knowledge lies in self-appropriation, namely in becoming aware of one's own processes of knowledge and in articulating them clearly to oneself. In this, his guide is Thomas Aquinas, but where Thomas worked from the outside to the inside, Lonergan, as a modern man, begins empirically and existentially within the human subject and works outwards to being.

One of the fundamental discoveries for our purposes, which he makes in this activity, is his analysis of the process of abstraction by which concepts are formed. According to the standard rational psychology, abstraction is an unconscious activity of the mind, producing concepts which then become the medium of our understanding. According to Lonergan, conceptualization is a conscious activity: concepts are produced *because* we understand. The process of conceiving issues from a prior act of understanding ('insight'), which is received in the mind as the agent intellect lights up the intelligibility contained within the phantasm. What this obscure point immediately contributes to our problem is an undermining of the notion of the beatific vision as a kind of mirror image of another world. For Lonergan, this vision is an act of understanding, of an essentially higher order than that of sensation such as is favoured by the image of a mirror. As understanding, it grasps things from the point of view of their unity, where unity comes before diversity.

More fundamentally, this analysis enables Lonergan to distance himself radically from the conceptualism which has been so influential in philosophy generally and in scholasticism in particular. At the beginning of this chapter we saw how Rahner transformed theology's approach to our whole question through his appreciation of a pre-conceptual element in knowledge. Lonergan moves in the same direction but goes even further. For Rahner the pre-conceptual element is the unthematic awareness of self which is the prior condition of all knowledge of objects. For Lonergan, as well as this self-awareness, there is a pre-conceptual element in every process of understanding in so far as concepts are formed in the light of a prior perceptual act, which Lonergan identifies as insight into phantasm: concepts are formed *because* we understand. It is this pre-conceptual element in all understanding which first embodies the specifically intellectual element in our knowing and marks it off from the processes proper to sensation.

Here we come to Lonergan's criticism of the cognitional theory of a broad swathe of philosophers, one which can win him few friends among those who disagree with him. It is a criticism which is so radical that it can only be seen as either presumptuous or true. Realist philosophers generally will be confident that they can distinguish sense knowledge from intellectual knowledge and that they have overcome the naive realism of positivism and empiricism. Not so, says Lonergan, as long as they have not appreciated the pre-conceptual nature of understanding. In Lonergan's terms, these thinkers have only incompletely extricated themselves from the naive realism they would wish to put behind them.

Again, from his point of view – and they would naturally dispute this – these philosophers interpret the process of knowing too closely on the model of sensation: knowing for them is basically 'taking a look'. If intellectual knowing is consequent on conceiving, it has to be ultimately a matter of taking a look at the content of a concept, which in turn mirrors the object to be understood. The 'real' is for them what he characterizes as the 'already-out-there-now-real', to be grasped by a process not sufficiently distinguished from sensation. The famous story of Samuel Johnson kicking a stone to establish its reality against Berkeley might be taken as a crude symbol of the kind of position Lonergan wishes to criticize. Though he associates this view with Scotus in particular, he assumes that it is present much more widely than Scotus and his school.

This analysis is relevant to the traditional discussion of the secondary objects of the beatific vision, namely the view by which the vision is held to embrace all actual realities, past, present and to come. Lonergan's interpretation helps to explain why this aspect of scholastic doctrine was much more of an embarrassment to the Scotist than to the Thomist school. For those who place understanding as consequent on conceiving there are two alternatives: either to reduce the vision of all actual realities to the realm of habitual knowledge, or to go all out for attributing to Jesus on earth a quasi-omniscience of the world in all its details. The former was the solution of Scotus himself; the latter was that of the 'Salmanticenses', namely of the Carmelite school of theology which flourished at Salamanca in the seventeenth century.

Lonergan's notion of the immediate vision as something prior to conceiving and to its being formulated in language identifies it with a mysterious and inarticulate grasp of the unity of all things in God. In no way does such a notion require us to attribute to the boy Jesus in the temple a capacity to lecture on Einstein's theory of relativity! The exalted nature of this grasp makes it in itself incommunicable. Lonergan here follows Aquinas in insisting that without the supplementing of his uncreated knowledge and of his vision of God with infused and acquired species, our Lord would have been unable to communicate any supernatural knowledge to the world.[53] It is only as one comes to appreciate the chasm between knowledge by the immediate vision of God and knowledge by species, whether infused or acquired, that one can make sense of Lonergan's confident statement at the Toronto School of Theology in 1973: 'I have no difficulty in holding that Jesus had the beatific vision all his life long from infancy.'[54] On another occasion he said: 'I think the difficulties made against the beatific vision are silly.'[55]

Given this approach to the vision of God, Lonergan has little difficulty in accepting into his view of our Lord's life on earth the evidence of the limitations of ordinary living which can be gathered from the gospels. As already mentioned, he takes over from Rahner the expression 'immediate' vision rather than 'beatific' vision, since with Thomas he allows for a certain suspension of the overflowing joy which would be the normal consequence of the direct vision of God. He makes the point that this joy does not come about through any automatic efficient causality of the vision of God but rather according to the concrete plan of divine wisdom by which the fulfilment of what Christ is about comes only at the term of a process.[56] This leaves room for the reality of suffering and anguish during Christ's life on earth, in particular during the passion, but it also allows for moments of transfiguration and mystical experience, such as may reasonably be expected to have occurred in the case of Jesus.[57]

As regards the role of infused knowledge and acquired knowledge in our Lord's ordinary life, Lonergan proposes the classical Thomistic account. His analysis of the processes of knowing makes him all the more appreciative of Aquinas' point that, far from making other levels of knowledge superfluous, Christ's higher gifts of knowledge stand in need of these other levels, if the message of revelation is to be conveyed to the world. Consequently, as regards acquired knowledge for instance, Lonergan is not that different from Rahner in his account of how our Lord, knowing things on one level, still has need of concrete searching and experience in order to articulate his response on the level of ordinary interchange. The author points to John 2:4 and to John 7:6f as possible illustrations of just such a transition from ineffable knowledge to an expression of acquired knowledge.[58] As regards the range of secondary objects of the vision, in light of the principle of a special dispensation, as outlined in the preceding paragraph, it is quite conceivable to think of these being restricted to an extent, if that seems necessary for one's account of Christ's life, though in fact this point is not made by Lonergan himself.[59]

The distinctiveness of Lonergan's approach is best brought out when one moves on to the question of Christ's consciousness as something other than his knowledge. This very distinction is one not as clearly made by other theologians as Lonergan makes it. For him, consciousness, in the strict sense of the term, is the self-awareness of the knowing subject as subject, whereas knowledge is an awareness of objects which is brought to completion by human beings in understanding and judgement. Though knowledge is indeed conscious, consciousness is not defined from knowing objects. It arises from the way the subject's awareness of the subject *as subject* is the condition of knowing any object.

This way of conceiving consciousness is relevant to one aspect of this whole problem which is not commonly commented on. It concerns Rahner's famous distinction between the non-thematic and the thematic. What is the real import of this distinction? In Rahner and in many of those dependent on him it seems to refer simply to the occurrence or non-occurrence of the *expression* of a content in concepts and propositions, whether verbally or merely internally. It is worth pointing out that in Lonergan the corresponding distinction usually has a much fuller meaning, referring as it does to the occurrence or non-occurrence of the relevant acts of understanding and judging, to which appropriate expression is then given, either externally or merely internally. It marks therefore a passage from the merely experiential level of consciousness to that of knowledge as such, underlining the difference between the two.

Already on the basis of this notion of consciousness as experience the difference between Lonergan and Rahner is becoming clearer.[60] Since the latter's distinction of knowledge from consciousness is not always as sharp as it might be, he locates Christ's immediate vision of God within his self-awareness. Consequently, as a function of his self-consciousness, it becomes focused on the Word of God rather than on the Father. For Lonergan, on the other hand, the vision of God is an act of *knowledge*, so that the difficult issue of Christ's awareness of himself and of his own divinity has to be handled differently.

In Christ there are two levels of consciousness, divine and human, each corresponding to the two natures, two intellects and two wills, but it is the one person, basically the one ego, who is conscious of self, on one level in a divine way, on another level in a human way.[61] This is the framework within which the crucial topic of Christ's awareness of his own divinity comes to be treated. For Rahner this was the central issue that determined all the rest. Having located the direct vision of the divinity within Christ's self-awareness, Rahner felt he had done justice to a central requirement of the magisterium, while his distinction between basic and reflexive consciousness, as explained above, enabled him to do justice to a contemporary 'theology from below'.

Lonergan treats the matter somewhat differently. For him, too, self-awareness is part of our primordial, inarticulate field of consciousness, but it is defined over against any subject–object relationship. The 'ego' which appears in Christ's human consciousness may in fact be identical with a divine person, but the fact that it is divine is precisely that, *a fact*, which can be known only as the object of judgement. Hence our Lord's awareness of his own nature as a divine nature is not exactly a matter of consciousness, in Lonergan's narrow sense of that term, but is a result of a combination of consciousness and of Christ's direct vision of the divinity. Through human consciousness one might, as in the case of Christ, be conscious of a divine person, but not of the divine nature, since it was a divine person who became incarnate, not a divine nature. To imply such a consciousness of the divine nature, as Rahner seems to do, is to indulge in an undue mingling of the natures. Is there here in Rahner a momentary slip into the Monophysitism he was always so concerned to avoid? This grasp of the divinity by the man Jesus is an act of knowledge requiring the immediate vision of God; but it also requires his own human consciousness if he is to grasp it as *his* divinity.[62]

We have already seen how Rahner has been criticized for not fitting in naturally with the data of the gospel, where our Lord's attitude to the divinity is presented as focused on the Father rather than on the Word of God. Lonergan's account of consciousness adapts much more easily to this exegetical perspective. Indeed he is more ready than many to take as historical the general lines of the Fourth Gospel, where Jesus speaks of God as Father, rejecting any dichotomy between Jesus' relationship to his heavenly Father and the Word's relationship to the First Person of the Trinity, while preserving the distinction of the two relationships.[63] In this he is somewhat closer to Balthasar, not least in that the Swiss theologian plays down the significance of Jesus' self-awareness, insisting that it never becomes an object for Jesus. In Christ's human mind, according to Balthasar, his hypostatic union with the Word is never a theme in its own right: 'The form of his human self-awareness is the *expression*, in terms of this world, of his eternal consciousness as Son.'[64]

Like Balthasar, Lonergan places obedience to the Father at the centre of Christ's relationship to God. In this he allows a certain room for the notion of Christ's faith, even in an intellectualist sense of that word. The immediate vision of God is not a knowledge of all possible reality, since that would be infinite. Consequently, even with this sublime knowledge, Christ's human mind remains in the dark as to why God chose *this* order of things, which includes his own suffering and death, rather than any other. Endowed, as he is, with the immediate vision of his Father, he must *obey*.[65] If Balthasar writes more existentially of the significance of this obedience, Lonergan concentrates on justifying it metaphysically.[66] His explanation includes the notion that the ordaining will of the divinity and the accepting human will of Jesus are, in a sense, like two sides of the one coin.[67] Balthasar has a parallel, though not identical, perception expressed in the following terms: 'In the self-same act in which he receives himself (and hence his divine understanding), he receives, too, the entire will of the Father concerning God and the world, and assents to it as his own.'[68]

*Conclusion*

Looking over these three writers on Christ's consciousness, despite the differences between them, one can discern certain common lines of approach. Each of them is content to work within the parameters of the Chalcedonian framework on Christology. Each of them feels he has done justice to Christ's transcendent grasp of his own divine personhood, but at the same time each wishes to accept the reality of Christ's limited knowledge and the notion of his human development. In this way we see how the advent of a more existential kind of theology has enabled Catholic scholars to marry the traditional confession of Christ's divinity with concern for the reality of Christ's humanity in a way which is more subtle than that which was commonly advanced in the theology of an earlier time. Readers will have their preferences among the various theologies we have described. The author will indicate his own view in the final chapter of this book.

NOTES

1  Rahner's first essay on this topic appeared in *Das Konzil von Chalkedon*, ed. A. Grillmeier and H. Bacht, vol. III (Würzburg: Echterverlag, 1954), now translated as 'Current Problems in Christology',TI 1 (1961), pp. 168–74. His main contribution came in a lecture to the Theological Faculty of Trier in 1961, now available as 'Dogmatic Reflections on the Knowledge and Self-Consciousness of Christ', TI 5 (1966), pp. 193–215. Also useful is the Christological section in *Foundations of Christian Faith*. For the importance of this discussion even for Protestant theology, see Pannenberg, *Jesus God and Man*, p. 328, and the latter's whole approach, *ibid.*, pp. 328–34.

2  Rahner considered that modernism devalued concepts in an unacceptable way: *Foundations*, p. 15.

3  For Rahner on the possibility of an orthodox 'consciousness Christology', see *Foundations*, pp. 302–4.

4  TI 5 (1966), p. 199. Against the suggestion of a kind of schizophrenic consciousness, Rahner feels he can reject the charge of an 'artificial layer-psychology' (*Stockwerkpsychologie*), given the unity of human subjectivity grounded in basic consciousness: *ibid.*, p. 203. This contrasts with the way medievalists rebut a parallel charge with an appeal to the objectivity and unity of the mind's formal object, being: Wéber, *Le Christ*, p. 201. For an example of an author where the charge of an artificial layer-psychology seems valid, see J. Maritain, *On the Grace and Humanity of Jesus* (London: Burns & Oates, 1969), pp. 47–61.

5  TI 5 (1966), pp. 201, 208–9.

6  TI 1 (1961), p. 170, n. 2.

7 Aquinas, ST III, q. 15, a. 5, obj. 3; q. 46, a. 8.
8 TI 5 (1966), p. 203. A reference to quasi-formal causality is made in this article on p. 205. The idea is explained at more length in 'Some Implications of the Scholastic Concept of Uncreated Grace', TI 1 (1961), pp. 319–46.
9 Rahner, *Foundations*, p. 200.
10 TI 1 (1966), p. 56; TI 21 (1988), pp. 210–11.
11 See K. Rahner, *The Love of Jesus and the Love of Neighbour* (Slough: St Paul's Publications, 1983), pp. 44–6.
12 TI 5 (1966), p. 204.
13 *Ibid.*, pp. 199 and 205.
14 *Ibid.*, p. 205. See also Rahner, *Foundations*, p. 303. Some scholars consider that this principle, as interpreted by Rahner, owes more to German idealism than to classical Thomism.
15 TI 5 (1966), p. 206. A purely ontic union would be one without consciousness.
16 Above, Chapter 5.
17 TI 5 (1966), pp. 207–9.
18 *Ibid.*, p. 213; also TI 1 (1961), p. 158.
19 Riedlinger, *Geschichtlichkeit und Vollendung*, pp. 152–3; Kasper, *Jesus the Christ*, p. 271, n. 60; D. Wiederkehr in *Mysterium salutis*, ed. J. Feiner et al. (Einsiedeln: Benziger, 1970), vol. III, 1, pp. 561f; p. 572, n. 86; p. 594, n. 106. See also Pannenberg, *Jesus God and Man*, p. 332. We might note Rahner's later friendly refusal of Kasper's criticisms in TI 21 (1988), p. 231.
20 E.g. TI 11 (1974), p. 194; TI 21 (1988), pp. 222–3. In the latter page Rahner says that the human soul of Jesus 'contemplates in adoration from an infinite distance of creatureliness', having earlier in the same essay placed the Word on the other side of that infinite divide: *ibid.*, p. 214.
21 TI 5 (1966), p. 213.
22 In this concept the English translation is misleading when it translates the original 'unthematisch' with 'implicit': TI 5 (1966), p. 213, translating *Schriften zur Theologie*, vol. V (Einsiedeln: Benziger, 1962), p. 243. The word 'implicit' in English does not clearly specify the relevant knowledge as actual, which is part of that which Rahner wished to convey.
23 In this way Rahner considers, as mentioned above, that he has done justice to the requirements of the magisterium on the matter. His account has been criticized for reintroducing 'a relative omniscience' by the back door: Riedlinger, *Geschichtlichkeit und Vollendung*, pp. 152–3.
24 TI 5 (1966), pp. 213–14.
25 TI 16 (1979), pp. 188–9; Rahner, *Foundations*, p. 250. J. McDermott considers that Rahner's position here undermines Christ's revelatory role: 'The Christologies of Karl Rahner', *Gregorianum* 67 (1986), p. 316.
26 The works referred to by these lists of names will be found in the bibliography.

27 H. U. von Balthasar, *The Glory of the Lord: A Theological Aesthetics*, in seven volumes (Edinburgh: T. & T. Clark, 1982–9); *Does Jesus Know Me? Do We Know Him?* (San Francisco: Ignatius Press, 1983); *A Theology of History* (London: Sheed & Ward, 1964); *Theodrama: Theological Dramatic Theory*, vol. III: *Dramatis Personae: The Person in Christ* (San Francisco: Ignatius Press, 1992), referred to below as *Theodrama*.

28 Balthasar, *Theodrama*, pp. 208–20.

29 *Ibid.*, p. 172. 'Comprehensor' refers to a person with the beatific vision, normally in the next life, while 'viator' refers to a person still involved in the journey of this life on earth.

30 E.g. Balthasar, *Theodrama*, p. 161. Notice that he follows Rahner's lead in speaking of an immediate vision rather than of a beatific vision: *ibid*, p. 166.

31 Balthasar, *The Glory of the Lord*, vol. VII, p. 144.

32 Balthasar, *A Theology of History*, p. 32.

33 In this Balthasar embraces the criticisms against this aspect of Rahner voiced by Riedlinger, *Geschichtlichkeit und Vollendung*, pp. 152–3; see Balthasar, *Theodrama*, pp. 172f.

34 Balthasar, *Theodrama*, p. 173.

35 *Ibid.*, p. 226. Cf. Balthasar, *A Theology of History*, p. 27.

36 Balthasar, *Theodrama*, p. 172. Cf. Balthasar, *A Theology of History*, pp. 27f.

37 Balthasar, *Theodrama*, p. 166.

38 *Ibid.*, p. 197.

39 *Ibid.*, p. 92.

40 *Ibid.*, p. 96, n. 84. Surely Balthasar here underestimates the gap between how Christ himself understood his words and how those who reported them understood them.

41 On this score Balthasar criticizes the well-known influential study by Voegtle on Christ's consciousness: *Theodrama*, p. 101, n. 95. For Voegtle's essay, see the Bibliography.

42 Balthasar, 'Fides Christi: an essay on the consciousness of Christ', *Spouse of the Word* (Explorations in Theology, no. 2; San Francisco: Ignatius Press, 1991), pp. 43–79.

43 This contrast, of course, is found in a number of places in the New Testament: John 20:19; 2 Cor 5:7; 1 Pet 1:8; cf. Rom 8:24.

44 Balthasar, *Theodrama*, p. 171. In an earlier discussion, Balthasar's treatment of the difficulty was less straightforward: *Spouse of the Word*, pp. 64–73.

45 *Theodrama*, p. 171, n. 11.

46 *Spouse of the Word*, p. 63.

47 An interesting example of a Catholic exegete inspired by Balthasar into exploring this hypothesis in the New Testament is J. Guillet, *La foi de Jésus-Christ* (Paris: Desclée, 1980).

48 G. O'Collins, *Christology*, pp. 250–68.

49 E.g. Jean Galot, *Who is Christ?* (Rome: Gregorian University Press, 1980), pp. 380, 382.

50 For Lonergan's view of Christ's knowledge, see *De Verbo incarnato*,

third edition (Rome: Gregorian University Press, 1964), pp. 332–416; *idem, De constitutione Christi ontologica et psychologica* (Rome: Gregorian University Press, 1961). Also useful are the articles by Crowe and Mansini referred to in Chapter 5 above. For Lonergan's response to being labelled a transcendental Thomist, see *Caring about Meaning*, ed. P. Lambert *et al.* (Toronto: Thomas More Institute, 1982), p. 68.

51 Lonergan, *De Verbo incarnato*, p. 354.
52 B. J. F. Lonergan, *Insight: A Study of Human Understanding* (London: Longmans, Green & Co., 1957).
53 In his article on Aquinas, Torrell agrees that this is Aquinas' view: 'S. Thomas d'Aquin', p. 400.
54 This unpublished lecture is preserved on tape and may be consulted in any one of the several Lonergan Centres, such as that in Milltown Park, Dublin.
55 Lonergan, Toronto Summer School on Method in Theology, Toronto 1969 (unpublished manuscript available for consultation at any of the Lonergan Centres), vol. 2, p. 606.
56 Lonergan, *De Verbo incarnato*, p. 340.
57 Crowe, 'Eschaton and worldly mission', p. 117. Cf. Balthasar, *Theodrama*, p. 197.
58 Lonergan, *De Verbo incarnato*, pp. 409f. Notice that where Rahner speaks of non-thematic and thematic consciousness Lonergan speaks of ineffable and effable knowledge.
59 I am indebted here to the late John Hyde SJ, though the point is made in a more radical way by Crowe, 'Eschaton and worldly mission', pp. 114, 118.
60 For a more detailed discussion of the difference between Rahner and Lonergan, see R. Moloney, 'The mind of Christ in transcendental theology: Rahner, Lonergan and Crowe', *Heythrop Journal* 25 (1984), pp. 288–300.
61 Lonergan, *De constitutione Christi*, pp. 89–95. The unity of the 'ego' in Christ will be discussed in more detail in the next chapter.
62 Lonergan, *De Verbo incarnato*, p. 309.
63 *Ibid.*, pp. 388–9.
64 Balthasar, *A Theology of History*, p. 28, author's italics.
65 Lonergan, *De Verbo incarnato*, p. 400. In a casual remark, made originally in conversation around the same time as the third edition of *De Verbo incarnato*, Lonergan said that as man Christ believed as much as we do. This seems to go further than the view expressed in his published work of the time, but since he never developed the point, the precise meaning of the remark remains unclear. The remark is found on the same page as that referred to at n. 55 of this chapter.
66 *Ibid.*, pp. 427–43.
67 Lonergan's technical expression for this is that precept and obedience occur 'in the simultaneous sign of truth', *De Verbo incarnato*, pp. 434ff. Behind this phrase lies a complicated metaphysical analysis of the relationship between Creator and creation which will not be

entered into here. For an explanation see Lonergan, *De constitutione Christi*, pp. 51–6; 63–5.

68  Balthasar, *A Theology of History*, p. 27. A further exposition of Lonergan's views on Christ's consciousness, especially as expressed by him in opposition to those put forward by P. Schoonenberg, has been left to the next chapter.

# 8

# ⊠ *Consciousness*

At various times in the course of this work, reference has been made to the question of Christ's consciousness, and in particular to the reality of his consciousness as a living human being. This topic is a particularly difficult one, since there is so little agreement among scholars even as to the meaning of the word itself. On the one hand there are those who present the phenomenon as a matter of interacting neurones;[1] on the other there is the lack of consensus among philosophers, ranging from those who see it as fundamental to those who regard it as not worthy of attention.[2] Since these are issues which cannot be solved in a book such as this, the method adopted here will lie in approaching the topic from within contemporary theology, and in particular from the transcendental philosophy and theology of some of the principal writers who have figured in this book.

The issue of consciousness has been brought to the centre of christological debate by a shift of emphasis in the way the notion of person and personhood is approached in contemporary thought. Throughout the classical and medieval periods personhood was understood in what was basically an ontological way, though the degree of explicitation of its metaphysical import may have varied. In modern philosophy, stemming from changes going back to Descartes and Locke, a new notion of personhood has become current. Though there is no agreement among scholars as to a precise definition of the concept, it is commonly assumed that consciousness and freedom are central to what people mean by 'person' today. Clearly this raises particular issues in the context of the Chalcedonian formula. The question immediately arises as to how one fits the aspect of consciousness into the dialectic between person and nature as these terms were understood at Chalcedon.

Sometimes the problem today is framed in terms of how, or to what extent, Jesus of Nazareth was conscious of his divine personhood and nature. Another common approach is concerned with the reality of human personality and consciousness in Jesus. The difficulty of both questions is brought to a head when one recalls a key contribution made at the Second Council of Constantinople when it clarified Chalcedon's use of 'one person' as referring to the divine person of the trinitarian Word.

This clarification has engendered among church theologians a certain reluctance to speak of 'human person' in the case of Christ. In this view Christ's human nature comes to subsistence and personhood only through the divine person who is the Eternal Word – a doctrine commonly given the technical name *enhypostasia*.[3] However, once personhood comes to be expressed in terms of consciousness and freedom, this traditional reluctance becomes more difficult to maintain. It is far from clear how one can vindicate any reality in Christ's humanity if one denies him a human consciousness and freedom. Behind this problem lies the question of what consciousness really means and of how it relates to the traditional terms of person and nature.

Unfortunately, as with person, so with consciousness, there is no generally agreed definition of its meaning. As a starting-point, one might describe it as 'self-awareness'. Commonly this is understood as knowledge of self, but already this interpretation can easily go astray. Knowledge is a structure which unfolds in questions and answers – questions for understanding unfolding in insights and concepts, questions for verification unfolding in judgements of reality. This process can be exercised on oneself as object just as much as on any other reality. When so focused, it can appropriately be termed introspection.

But introspection is not consciousness. Introspection is part of the superstructure which is knowledge. Consciousness is something logically prior and more primitive, part of an infrastructure which knowledge presupposes. All knowledge is a response in questioning and answering to experience, whether internal or external. Consciousness is an aspect of internal experience. It is not the subject's awareness of the subject as an object. It is the subject's awareness of the subject *as subject.*

In one way consciousness is less than knowledge and introspection: it is simply a matter of experience, whereas they are matters of understanding and affirming. In another way it is more than knowledge. Knowledge simply discovers reality, and by definition leaves its object unchanged. Consciousness is constitutive of reality: it moves the subject from being unconscious to conscious, and so leads it into a new level of activity and attainment. Consciousness is that element in our conscious activity by which we are aware that it is *we* who are carrying out this activity.

With this analysis one can face the question as to how consciousness fits into the christological dialectic of person and nature. Commonly consciousness is seen as a function of nature. If there are two levels of nature in Christ, then there are two levels of consciousness as well. For each of these latter levels I will sometimes use the more convenient word 'subjectivity'. However consciousness, as self-awareness, has something to do with one's own *ego*; so if consciousness is to be doubled in Christ, we are left with a question as to whether there are two *egos* in him.

This particular issue arose in theology just before the Second World War. An emphasis on the side of duality is associated with two scholars in particular, Déodat de Basly and Léon Seiller. The latter wrote once: 'God the Word is the subject adored, in no way the subject adoring ... the subject prayed to, in no way the subject praying.' The work in which this statement appeared was placed on the Index of Forbidden Books.[4]

As a representative of an opposite emphasis, and one that fits more easily than the foregoing into traditional orthodoxy, we might consider the view of Jean Galot. Every explanation, he writes, should take as its starting-point, not the human being in Christ, but the divine person in a human existence.[5] Galot is clear that consciousness is, in the first place, a function of the person, but of that person, in the case of Christ, functioning in two natures. Consequently one of the first points to be made establishes a clear distinction between divine consciousness and human consciousness, in line with the principle of duality without commingling, as taught by the Third Council of Constantinople.[6]

Galot goes on from there to formulate the problem of Christ's consciousness in terms of the 'I'. Is there in Christ a human 'I' alongside the divine 'I', a human subject alongside the divine subject? When faced with this question, particularly in reaction to the work of de Basly and Seiller, theologians generally make it clear that there can be only one ontological subject in Christ, the divine person, though the thesis of two 'psychological subjects' is considered doctrinally possible.[7] Not surprisingly, in the light of his position outlined above, Rahner has led many along this path of the two subjects, and inveighs against what he calls 'Monosubjectivism'.[8] Galot allows some reality to the notion of a 'human I' in Christ in so far as the operations of consciousness are inevitably coloured by the nature within which they occur; but ultimately he insists that when people speak of their 'I' they are speaking of the person.[9] Consequently the 'I' of Christ's human consciouness is the divine person of the Word in a human psychology.[10] On the other hand Galot maintains that 'the "I" of Christ cannot be referred solely to the divinity'. 'It cannot be claimed that this "I" is the "I" of God in the unity of his nature.' 'He behaves *vis-à-vis* the Father as an "I" confronting a "You".'[11]

Another way of approaching the question of Christ's consciousness starts from Christ humanity and human consciousness. The premise of this approach is the insistence on the full reality of his humanity, and consequently on the full reality of his human consciousness. The point at issue concerns how this is related to the aspect of 'person' in him. Norman Pittenger is representative of this approach when he defines person as 'the psychological centre of subjective experience'. This leads him into a denial of the doctrine which lay behind the principle summed up in the term *enhypostasia*: 'It is not really possible to maintain true manhood while at the same time finding for that manhood no creaturely centre; if the Word in any way takes the place of that centre, instead of working in and through it, we are on the road to a revival of the Eutychian heresy.'[12]

While this approach might well lay claim to being the

majority view within Protestant theology, at least in an implicit way, in Catholic theology it has been taken up only by a minority, since the authority of the ancient councils seems to exclude it. One of the best-known names in that minority is the Dutch theologian, Piet Schoonenberg, whose views on our question are very similar to those of Norman Pittenger. The Dutchman's starting-point is 'the modern notion of person', where, he tells us, consciousness and freedom are to the forefront.[13] As we have seen above, this is not what was intended by the word in the classical tradition, where the focus was on the ontological ground of subjective experience. If one wishes to keep the word *person* for this ontological notion, the word *personality* might be used loosely for this 'modern notion of person'.[14] Much of our problem with the classical formulae of Christology lies in the confusion between these two aspects of the issue.

In the meantime Schoonenberg has not hesitated to go to the heart of the problem and to reject the classical doctrine according to which, if Nestorianism is to be kept at bay, the ultimate personal centre of the life and consciousness of Jesus has to be found, not in his humanity, but in the Divine Word who is incarnate there. Schoonenberg disagrees: 'Here we are concerned with his (Christ's) humanity and his personhood. These must unhesitatingly be awarded to Christ. For what does it mean if one denies in him a human created act of being? This Jesus is no longer a man.'[15]

For Schoonenberg it is clear that in Christ there is only one person, but he is so convinced of the complete humanity of Jesus that he considers that this 'person' must be understood in terms of *human* personhood and consciousness. In this way he turns on its head the traditional doctrine which speaks of the subsistence of the human nature in the divine person. He prefers to speak rather of the subsistence of the divine nature in the human person, and he calls this in one place 'enhypostasis in reverse'.[16] The existence of an individual human centre of acts, decision and self-consciousness alongside the divine person of the Word and, as it were, in competition with it, is rejected by him.[17] The human ego or act-centre of Jesus, he maintains, cannot be considered as real unless grounded in the one ontological person, which in this case can only be the human person,

Jesus of Nazareth. 'If in Jesus Christ the human ego or act-centre stands psychologically outside his ontological person, it is then clearly not the ego or act-centre of Jesus.'[18]

One of the notable points about Schoonenberg's thesis is that it was the occasion for a vigorous reply by Bernard Lonergan in which he gave us one of the principal statements of his Christology from the period of his mature thought.[19] In outlining the Canadian's reply to his Dutch confrère we will see that consciousness is a point of intersection for some of the key issues of Christology generally, and so a description of this debate enables us to set out some of the key ontological concepts underlying the basic topic of this book.

An important strength of Lonergan's position lies in the clarification it brings to the distinction between the ontological and the psychological aspects, which are so intertwined in these complex questions. Lonergan is clear that the two natures in Christ have to be matched by two distinct levels of consciousness, the human and the divine, though, as pointed out in a previous chapter,[20] these are both grounded in an 'ego' which is ultimately one. The question of divine consciousness may be left to the theology of the Trinity, but for Christology it is significant that Christ's human consciousness can be seen to establish a field of awareness with its own kind of unity, and with a psychological centre which has a meaning different from that traditionally ascribed to the classical ontological notion of person.

The issue might be highlighted by considering the meaning of the word 'one', as when we speak of Christ as *one and the same*, or of his consciousness as having *one* psychological centre. There are, in fact, three meanings that can be distinguished:

> (a) The 'one' of number, like numbering cars of the same make rolling off an assembly line. This kind of unity occurs when things are understood in basically the same way; the difference is purely material.

> (b) The 'one' of formal unity, as found when things are understood in basically different ways, like when we distinguish cars from motorbikes, or, better, animals from plants. The basis of such unity, at least in the second example, is the substantial form, known by an act of understanding.

(c) The 'one' of actual identity, as given where a reality is judged to be itself and not anything else. Such
an identity is grasped by affirmation and negation,
when the principles of identity and non-contradiction
are found to be verified in a given instance. The metaphysical basis of such a judgment is the act of being,
*esse*.[21]

The kernel of Lonergan's contribution to our problem, as
it was the kernel of his reply to Schoonenberg, lies in his distinction between the 'one' of formal unity and the 'one' of
actual identity. To each of these senses he gives, not only a
different metaphysical base (form as distinct from act), but
a different epistemological one (understanding as distinct
from judgement); and armed with this distinction he can
vindicate the unity of Christ's human psychological development on the one hand, and the identity of his personhood
on the other. For those who discount metaphysics, these distinctions will doubtless seem like 'theology overreaching
itself in speculation',[22] but for those who find them helpful,
they are like the tweezers of the scientist, helping to hold
apart what otherwise would be confused.

For our purposes the principal interest in this approach
lies in the possibility it gives us of appreciating the unity of
Christ's conscious activity without trespassing on the question of his personhood. Problems of the development of
Christ's consciousness and knowledge are questions about
his human subjectivity. Subjectivity is an area of diversity
and development. All the richness of human psychology can
be found there. Even the sense in which the human ego is
said to develop is to be accounted for on this level.[23] But
clearly this subjectivity must have some principle of unity
proper to itself. The diversity of acts in our conscious activities are not total confusion. Lonergan's contribution lies in
giving some account of the unity of subjectivity without
involving immediately the personhood on which it is ultimately based.

Subjectivity is defined by him as 'the intelligible unity in
the multi-dimensional manifold of the conscious events of
a life-time'.[24] This is the 'one' of formal unity, the kind of
unity grasped by an act of understanding. Just as behind all
the diversity of the moon's phases, the understanding can

discern a unity which we call the sphericity of the moon, so too there is a unity proper to the level of subjectivity. It is natural that the conscious events within subjectivity should have a central focus. This is what Lonergan referred to once as 'the human centre of consciousness' or 'the psychological centre of our conscious activity'.[25]

The metaphysical basis of this unity is the principle of being, referred to in *Insight* as 'central form', but more familiar to scholastic philosophy as the substantial form of a human nature. The unity referred to in Chalcedon's 'one and the same' is a unity on another level, as different from the former as existence is different from essence, judgement from understanding, person from nature, act from form. What Schoonenberg does not allow for is that the unity of our conscious activity is not the unity we refer to when we speak of person, subject and identity in Christ. Since the human nature remains integral in the incarnation, there is no difficulty in seeing this human centre of consciousness still present in Christ. In this way Lonergan has a metaphysical and epistemological basis for being open to all that a modern notion of personality might wish to find in one who is 'like us in all things but sin'. But Lonergan is clear that phenomenology is not enough. In the long run one has to speak of person and identity, distinguishing them from central form.

The question of Christ's personhood and identity is also illuminated by Lonergan's approach. All the activity of human consciousness and knowledge has to be grounded ultimately in an act of existence, distinct from essence, form and nature. As well as the psychological centre of conscious activity, there is the identity that carries on that activity through that centre. At this point Lonergan passes from the level of 'nature' to that of 'person', taking those terms in their classical scholastic sense. In his later period, however, Lonergan more usually speaks of identity rather than of person. He tells us that this notion of identity is sufficient to express what Chalcedon held to be one in Christ. Again he says that the doctrine of the Trinity teaches three identities in God, though to go on to describe them as relations, in the way scholasticism likes to do, is saying something more.[26]

When viewed in this light we can see that many of our

problems in this area arise, not only by confusing what is to be distinguished, but by not appreciating that person in its classical sense, and 'personality' in its modern sense, do not represent two rival accounts of the one reality. They are really dealing with two different levels of reality altogether, and indeed the level to which the classical notion of person belongs simply lies beyond the horizon of many of those who wish to take up these problems today.

Baron von Hügel once used the phrase 'unincarnate Word' in order to contrast the hidden infinity of the divine Person with the finite conditions of his existence in the flesh. This illustrates how easily, in speaking of this mystery, one can slip from person to nature without realizing it. Perhaps this helps us to appreciate the point of Lonergan's insistence that 'nature' is known through understanding, whereas 'person' is known through judgement. The content of that judgement is an affirmation of identity and nothing more. This identity remains itself and can be affirmed, whatever the nature in which it exists. Whether the person is found in a divine nature or a human nature, in either or in both, is a completely separate question, to be answered only by appreciating the situation in which that person exists. It was not the divine nature which became incarnate but simply the person who in heaven exists in a divine nature.

Schoonenberg was criticized by more than Lonergan, and in fact it is not easy to see how his position can be reconciled with the teachings of the Second and Third Councils of Constantinople. However it is only fair to remark that Schoonenberg later explained his position in a more nuanced way, though an assessment of his later views lies beyond the scope of this chapter.[27] Enough has been said to show the relevance of these ancient concepts to contemporary debate and, above all, to establish a distinction between person and consciousness, which is so helpful in dealing with the issues of this book.

NOTES

1 See, for instance, *The Scientific American*, 267:3 (September 1992).
2 The topic is fundamental in J.P. Sartre, *Being and Nothingness* (London: Methuen, 1957), for instance in the Introduction, while Iris Murdoch could write at one stage, 'It is a subject which no longer

exists in British philosophy', *Existentialists and Mystics: Writings on Philosophy and Literature* (London: Chatto & Windus, 1997), p. 146.

3  This term *enhypostasia*, and its associated term, *anhypostasia*, which refers to the absence in Christ of a finite personhood correlative to his human nature, were developed in particular through a mistaken reading of the patristic sources. Nevertheless, the doctrine to which the terms refer is part of authentic tradition. For the original situation see Grillmeier, *Christ in Christian Tradition*, vol. II, 2, pp. 193–8; 282–6; 289–93. On the whole issue, see F. L. Shults, 'A dubious christological formula: From Leontius of Byzantium to Karl Barth', *Theological Studies* 57 (1996), pp. 431–46.

4  L. Seiller, *La psychologie humaine du Christ et l'unicité de personne* (Rennes–Paris: Vrin, 1950), p. 17. This work, published the previous year in *Franziskanische Studien* 31 (1949), pp. 49–76, 246–74, was placed on the Index of Forbidden Books by a decree of the Holy Office, 12 July 1951: AAS 43 (1951), p. 561. See also the condemnation of certain christological views by Pius XII, *Sempiternus Rex*: AAS 43 (1951), p. 638; ND 663; DS 3905.

5  J. Galot, *La coscienza di Gesù* (Assisi: Cittadella, 1974), p. 154. Galot criticizes Rahner for basing Christ's consciousness in the human nature and in the human soul rather than in the divine subject: see *ibid.*, pp. 152–4.

6  ND 636; DS 557. Thus Galot, *Who is Christ?*, p. 319. See the whole discussion *ibid.*, pp. 319–43.

7  Rahner, TI 1 (1961), pp. 159f.

8  Rahner, TI 11 (1974), pp. 198f. In an interview given in 1974 Rahner remarked: 'Perhaps it is possible to be an orthodox Nestorian or an orthodox Monophysite. If this were the case, I would prefer to be an orthodox Nestorian', *Karl Rahner in Dialogue: Conversations and Interviews 1965–1982*, ed. P. Imhof and H. Biallowons (New York: Crossroad, 1986), p. 127.

9  Galot, *Who is Christ?*, p. 329.

10  *Ibid.*, p. 331. Contrast Crowe: 'The immediate knowledge Jesus had of God did not include the word "I"', 'Eschaton and worldly mission', p. 119.

11  Galot, *Who is Christ?*, p. 334.

12  Pittenger, *The Word Incarnate*, p. 93. Macquarrie follows a similar line, *Jesus Christ*, p. 163.

13  Schoonenberg, *The Christ*, p. 78.

14  This terminology is suggested by the International Biblical Commission in reference to Schoonenberg. See Fitzmyer, *Scripture and Christology*, p. 5, para. 1.1.2.3.

15  Schoonenberg, *The Christ*, p. 73. For a similar line see F. J. van Beeck, *Christ Proclaimed: Christology as Rhetoric* (New York: Paulist Press, 1979), pp. 167–82.

16  Schoonenberg, *The Christ*, pp. 87, 90. For 'enhypostasis in reverse', see P. Schoonenberg, 'Antwoord aan P. Jean Galot', *Tijdschrift voor Theologie* 20 (1980), pp. 86–92, at p. 90.

17  Schoonenberg, *The Christ*, p. 65.

18 *Ibid.*, p. 70. Pittenger makes the point that if God is seen as replacing the operational centre of human life with his own 'person', that 'makes Jesus nothing more than a body manipulated as an external instrument for deity', *The Word Incarnate*, p. 95.

19 'Christology today: methodological reflections'. First published in 1976 among the papers of a colloquium at the University of Laval, Quebec, this paper is now available in *A Third Collection: Papers by Bernard Lonergan*, ed. F. Crowe (New York: Paulist, 1985; London: Chapman, 1985), pp. 74–99. For the significance of the reference in the text to 'his mature thought', see my article already referred to, *Heythrop Journal* (1984), p. 297.

20 See Chapter 7 above at n. 61 and reference there.

21 Lonergan, *A Third Collection*, p. 91; *A Second Collection*, p. 258.

22 The phrase is Macquarrie's concerning the doctrine of *anhypostasia*: *Jesus Christ*, p. 163.

23 'The ordinary child does not know the word "I" but has to learn to use it ... I see no reason for asserting anything different about Jesus', Crowe, 'Eschaton and worldly mission, p. 119.

24 Lonergan, 'Christology today', p. 98, n. 40.

25 Lonergan, Harvard Seminar on Christology, 1972. These lectures have not been published but are preserved on tape in any of the Lonergan Centres where they may be consulted, e.g. at the Dublin Lonergan Centre, Milltown Park, Dublin 6.

26 Lonergan, *A Second Collection*, pp. 258–9.

27 P. Schoonenberg, 'Het avontuur der christologie', *Tijdschrift voor Theologie* 12 (1972), pp. 307–32; *idem*, 'Antwoord aan P. Jean Galot', *Tijdschrift voor Theologie* 20 (1980), pp. 86–92, where he moves from 'enhypostasis in reverse' to a 'reciprocal enhypostasis', *ibid.*, p. 90.

# 9

⊠ *The modern magisterium*

In the chapter on the patristic period we have seen something of how the question of Christ's knowledge figured in the magisterium of the ancient Church. The evidence considered there was found to be somewhat sporadic, though it did play its part in forming that consensus against ignorance in Christ which has been an influence in the Church ever since. In modern times the issue did not become a significant one for the Church's teaching authority until it was raised in the context of modernism as the nineteenth century passed into the twentieth. Throughout the nineteenth century, the traditional synthesis on Christ's knowledge, which had been put together in the Middle Ages, was generally preserved intact in Roman Catholic schools, but at the turn of the century some cracks began to appear.

Alfred Loisy had been a professor at the Institut Catholique in Paris from 1884 to 1893. In 1902, to counter the individualism of Harnack, he published his defence of the notion of the Church, *L'Evangile et l'église*.[1] Stressing the aspect of development in the Church, Loisy declared that Jesus could never have foreseen what the Church would become. In later studies of the gospels he postulated an earthly Jesus unconscious of his own divinity. All this placed the question of Jesus' knowledge and consciousness right at the centre of Catholic theology.[2] The issue figured prominently in the official condemnations of modernism, but even more far-reaching was the ensuing paralysis of reflection on the matter which was to bedevil Catholic theology for the first four decades of the twentieth century.

An appreciation of this climate of fear and insecurity is a

necessary presupposition for estimating the dogmatic force of the various statements of the magisterium on the issue. This is a difficult, and even an embarrassing, question, which Catholic theology today cannot avoid, if its sense of responsibility is to embrace the past as well as the present. The principal documents are of two types, papal encyclicals and decrees of the Holy Office. Of the encyclicals, the most important was that of Pius X, *Pascendi dominici gregis* of 1907, dealing directly with the modernism of the time. As regards our question, this encyclical is concerned to reject the way the distinction between the Jesus of history and the Christ of faith might be used against any supernatural view of the psychology of the earthly Jesus.[3] Further encyclicals to touch on the matter were *Miserentissimus Redemptor* of Pius XI (1928) and *Mystici corporis Christi* of Pius XII (1943). In these the fact of Christ's beatific vision is clearly taught, and it is interpreted as an explicit knowledge of each individual believer.[4]

The decrees of the Holy Office are more precise. That of July 1907, *Lammentabili*, was devoted directly to the condemnation of modernism. In particular it condemned aspects of the notion of development as applied to Jesus' awareness of his messianic status.[5] The decree of 1918 was even more specific, rejecting as unsafe any denial of Christ's beatific vision while on earth. It interprets this vision as a knowledge of all things, past, present and future, excluding in that sense any ignorance in Christ.[6]

In some defence of these statements it can be granted that their overall thrust reflects the general consensus of the Catholic theologians of the day. They should also be related to the limited state of Catholic exegesis at the time, which had not yet experienced the biblical renewal, later to be ushered in by Pius XII with his encyclical, *Divino afflante Spiritu*.[7] Above all, they should be related to the climate of fear and confusion brought about by modernism itself. Many people realized that there was something seriously wrong in the modernist movement but they had not yet developed the theological and philosophical tools for sifting the wheat from the chaff amongst the various ideas being put forward. Not for the first time, the reaction of those in authority was the prudential one of reinforcing the safe

theories of the past, but it is important to underline that the
intervention of the magisterium did not invoke the ultimate
note of irreformable doctrine.

Anticipating somewhat the subject-matter of our next
chapter, one can say that, after an initial stage of paralysis
and negativity, Catholic theology gradually began to come to
grips with the issues raised by modernism. With the passage
of the years, new movements developed, not only with the
renewal of biblical studies, but in particular with the emergence of a more existentialist and personalist philosophy and
theology. With these developments, the climate changed,
and it became possible to see things in a new light, not only
the issues themselves, but the statements of the magisterium
surrounding them. In a theologian like Karl Rahner it is
always noticeable in his early writings how he has to distinguish himself from modernism, but it is also equally noticeable how he tries to bring his reflections on Christ's knowledge into line with the basic thrust of these statements of
the magisterium, while at the same time contributing in no
mean degree to their eventual replacement. We might also
notice his view that in the question of Christ's immediate
knowledge of God there is a point of doctrine which
Catholic theologians are not free to doubt.[8]

Questions of Christology were not a central concern at
the Second Vatican Council, so that there is no need to seek
guidance on these matters from its documents, but in one
incidental statement it does capture the mood of contemporary Christology in vindicating the humanity of Christ's
mind and heart: 'By his incarnation, the Son of God has in
some way united himself with each human being. He
laboured with human hands, he thought with a human
mind, he acted with a human will, and he loved with a
human heart.'[9] Vatican II, however, is significant for this
book in the new climate in theology to which it gave its
blessing. It was this new climate which facilitated theologians in seeking a new perspective on this as on so many
questions, so that, when the organs of the Holy See returned
to our topic in subsequent years, it was with a new openness
to Scripture and a new breadth of theological vision.

*Four Official Texts*

Over the past two decades four documents of the Holy See have dealt with questions of Christ's knowledge or related topics. Of these four documents, three have come from the International Theological Commission and one from the Pontifical Biblical Commission.[10] Though these commissions are not formally organs of the Church's teaching office, they represent a significant extension of the work of the Second Vatican Council and of the Synods of Bishops to which they owe their origin. Furthermore each commission is associated, through its president, with the Sacred Congregation for the Doctrine of the Faith. In this way they can be considered as taking the place, in the light of more recent scholarship, of the statements on these matters made earlier in the century by the commissions and congregations of the Roman Curia. As Cardinal Ratzinger said of the International Theological Commission, its contribution lies in 'gaining a hearing for the common voice of theology amid all the diversities that occur'.[11] The perspective in all four statements is somewhat wider than the specific concerns of this book, so it is a question of going through them to see what they have to say about the knowledge and consciousness of Christ.

The first statement, entitled 'Select Questions on Christology', was concluded in 1979 by the International Theological Commission.[12] One of the main concerns in this document is the question of the unity between Christology and soteriology. With this in mind it deliberately leaves untouched the issue of Christ's human consciousness, but it does reflect on aspects of his knowledge relevant to soteriology, in particular on how Christ understood his own life and death. Appealing to the evidence for Jesus' preaching of the kingdom, the document insists that Jesus knew himself to be the definitive Saviour of the Last Times. He understood his life as 'an existence for others', totally dedicated to live and die for God and his fellow human beings. The commission rejects the notion of Jesus being overtaken by death in a purely passive manner, overcome by a sense of abandonment by God. On the contrary he was aware of his death beforehand and prepared for it as the climax of his life of service, always confident in the ultimate triumph of the kingdom.

The commission's second statement, issued in 1981, was entitled 'Theology, Christology, Anthropology'. As the title suggests, this statement is concerned with the relationship of Christology to other theological treatises. It deliberately postpones from its purview questions of Christ's knowledge and consciousness, but its defence of the notion of Christ's pre-existence can be seen as preparation for a use of the same concept in the context of Christ's knowledge which will come up in the last of the four documents.[13]

In the same year, 1981, the statement of the Pontifical Biblical Commission on Scripture and Christology was published. It is a wide-ranging survey of the method and content of a biblical theology of Christ, in the course of which a few statements on knowledge and consciousness are made. The commission is concerned to combat the historical scepticism associated with Bultmann and insists that the origin of Christology has to be found, not just in the early community, but in the words and deeds of Jesus himself. It agrees with the International Theological Commission in grounding Christology in the way Jesus preached the kingdom, underlining the evidence for the notion that the kingdom was perceived as present in his person and work.[14] As this book has done in Chapter 3 above, the commission finds the ultimate secret of Christ's person and personality in his filial relationship to God, revealed especially in his *Abba* experience. Of this relationship Christ was conscious even at a young age, but, as the theological commission had already suggested, his consciousness of himself and of his mission is subject to a process of development and clarification from his childhood up to his death on the cross.[15]

The last of the four statements we are considering was the only one to deal directly with the topic of this book. It is entitled 'The Consciousness of Christ concerning Himself and His Mission', and was completed in 1985 by the International Theological Commission.[16] Taking account of the divisions which had arisen among theologians on these difficult matters, the commission wished to avoid the complexities of philosophy, and it chose instead to speak 'at the level of what the Faith has always believed about Christ'. It does this in four propositions, which may be summed up as follows:

a. Jesus was conscious of his own divine sonship.
b. Jesus knew that his mission was to announce the kingdom and to save the world.
c. Jesus willed the foundation of the Church.
d. Jesus was moved by love for all, and in some sense for each as in Galatians 2:20.

Though this statement comes from a theological commission, its commentary on each of these propositions does not go much further than invoking the biblical evidence in its support, but it does this in the light of the dogmatic-theological tradition. Thus the first proposition, which is the closest to the central subject-matter of this book, is traced back to the way Jesus called God his Father and to the consciousness this indicates of his own divine authority and mission. This fact is grounded, not only in the Fourth Gospel, but also in the Synoptics and in texts of the earliest apostolic preaching.

The evidence for the second proposition flows by natural progression from that for the first: unless Jesus knew that he was the Son, the emissary of the Father, both Christology and soteriology would lack foundation. Here the commentary includes an often neglected perspective, pointing to our Lord's relationship to the Spirit as well as to the Father. From his baptism on, all his work is brought about only in and through the Spirit.

The foundation of the Church is the issue in the third proposition, that Church which, from the earliest post-Easter preaching, has been inseparable from Christ. The will of the historical Jesus to found the Church is revealed, not so much in his determining all its later institutional aspects, though some of these do have a basis in determinations made by Jesus himself, but rather in his commitment to ensuring that all the world would enter the kingdom.

In its fourth proposition the commission gives its view concerning one of the most difficult issues in the whole discussion of Christ's knowledge, and also one of the most important ones if only because of its place in the history of spirituality. It is the question of Jesus' knowledge and love for each individual for whom he died. The commission makes clear that this knowledge and love of Christ is already

presented in the Pauline epistles as not just 'a general attitude' by which Christ would die for the people considered
simply as a collectivity. Already for Paul, and in subsequent
church life, it is understood 'as a concrete love expressed in
terms of personal consideration for every individual'.[17] This
aspect of Christ's love is one of the fundamental inspirations
of Christian spirituality, not only as underlining the value of
the least of Christ's little ones as 'one for whom Christ died'
(Rom 14:15), but also as stirring the hearts of countless individuals down the centuries to respond in a personal way to
this personal love of Christ for us.

When it comes to explaining this love, the commission's
response is significant as much for what it does not say as for
what it does. Previously when this issue had been treated in
an older theology and in papal encyclicals, an answer had
been sought in the notion of Christ's beatific vision, understood as a direct grasp of all actual realities, past, present
and to come. What is most significant in this 1985 statement
is that not a word is said about the beatific vision. Instead it
speaks of Christ's knowledge in three different 'stages' of his
being, namely in his pre-existence, in his life on earth and in
his reign in heaven after the resurrection. In explaining the
individualized love attributed to Christ in the New
Testament, the commission says that the apostolic witnesses
hold Christ's love in all three stages 'in a single glance', but
it underlines in particular the role of the pre-existent love as
being the continuing element in all three stages. It can be
seen from this that, though the statement leaves open the
question of the special human knowledge of the beatific
vision, it follows the example of the patristic writers in treating as decisive the divine knowledge of the Son of God, who
'received everything in eternity from God the Father'.[18]

In these four documents we have the main official statements from within the Church since the Second Vatican
Council on the question of Christ's knowledge and consciousness. While these statements are not formally documents of the magisterium, they do have a certain official
standing, given their source as set out above. Apart from
their own particular content, they have significance in that
they take the place of the statements of the Church on the
matter in the early decades of the twentieth century. In this

way they help to underline the time-conditioned nature of those earlier statements and they put an end to the embarrassment which those statements undoubtedly caused to scholars, who have been trying to see these matters in a new light. It seems to this writer that the points they make are minimal enough and leave a wide field of reflection open to the theologian and the exegete. Availing of this freedom, it only remains for me to indicate in a final chapter my personal views in the matter.

NOTES

1  A. Loisy, *The Gospel and the Church* (Philadelphia PA, 1976).
2  In this context we might note a remark of Blondel writing to J. Wehrlé in 1903: 'The *sensus fidelium* knows better than the scholars that to deny the divine consciousness of Jesus is to deny the divinity of Christ': cited by R. Marlé, *Au cœur de la crise moderniste* (Paris: Aubier, 1960), p. 78.
3  DS 3496.
4  AAS 20 (1928), pp. 171–4; 35 (1943), pp. 229–330. In a further encyclical of Pius XII, *Sempiternus Rex* (1951), the theory of kenoticism was roundly condemned, AAS 43 (1951), pp. 634–8.
5  DS 3427–38.
6  DS 3645–47.
7  AAS 35 (1943), pp. 309ff.
8  TI 5 (1966), p. 215.
9  Vatican II, *Gaudium et spes*, art. 22.
10  For these texts, see *International Theological Commission: Texts and Documents 1969–1985*, ed. M. Sharkey (San Francisco: Ignatius Press, 1989). For the document of the Biblical Commission see *Scripture and Christology: A Statement of the Biblical Commission with a Commentary*, translation and commentary by J. Fitzmyer (London: Chapman, 1986). These books will be referred to below by the surname of the editor in each case.
11  Foreword in Sharkey, p. viii.
12  For the text, see Sharkey, pp. 185–205.
13  For text see Sharkey, pp. 207–23; on Christ's pre-existence, see pp. 216–19.
14  Fitzmyer, p. 41.
15  Fitzmyer, p. 45. Cf. Sharkey, p. 198.
16  For text, see Sharkey, pp. 305–16.
17  Sharkey, p. 314.
18  This is to interpret the 1985 statement in the light of the Son's pre-existence as explained in the statement of 1981, from which the phrase cited here in this sentence is taken: Sharkey, p. 217.

# 10

## ⊠ *Immediacy to God in history*

In the preceding chapters of this book, the approach to the topic before us has largely lain through considering the opinions of others. Such a presentation is inevitably influenced by how the presenter sees the question; so in order to help my readers to assess the matter, it seems appropriate that in this, the final chapter, I should give some account of how I personally see our question in the light of all that has gone before.

The first point is one about method. Few would dispute today that the basic inspiration for any reflection on this topic has to lie in the data of the New Testament. The image of Christ which emerges from the gospels leaves one in no doubt as to the reality of his humanity, but it would be wrong to focus on this in a one-sided way. At this stage I would underline that the New Testament cannot answer our question on its own. I trust it has been made clear that the evidence to be gathered from that source is ambivalent, now favouring one side of the argument, now another. In so far as an eventual answer can be given at all, it can come only by taking the New Testament in combination with the subsequent dogmatic tradition. Indeed the only absolutely certain points in the whole matter are those few clear truths of church teaching on the unity and duality in Christ, which act as points of reference for any further reflection.

Despite indications of limitations in Christ's knowledge, the dominant picture of Jesus of Nazareth in his public life is of one who knew what he was about and who startled his contemporaries with the newness of his message. He always proclaimed the nearness of God's kingdom with an unwavering certainty as to the basic fact, and by that point alone was implicitly laying claim to a unique communication of knowledge between himself and God. This primary datum of historical research is then, of course, given new depth and significance when it is joined to the appreciation of his divine sonship in the early community. In this way the groundwork is prepared for the ebb and flow of subsequent christological reflection, as the Church, under the inspiration of the Holy Spirit, works out the implications of all this as to the nature and personhood of Christ on the one hand, and as to his knowledge and consciousness on the other.

It will surely be clear that in devoting so much space to the thought of the three authors, Rahner, Balthasar and Lonergan, I have been suggesting that the converging lines of their approaches point in the direction I myself would wish to take. The fundamental truth in the whole matter has to be, of course, the essential mysteriousness of the subject of our enquiry. One cannot recall too often the words of Mascall, quoted already in the first chapter above: 'It is both ridiculous and irreverent to ask what it must have been like to be God incarnate.' Another basic guideline has to be the fact that in Christ there are different levels of awareness. This is already a point where we can experience something analogous within ourselves, so that we can know things on one level and not know them on another. If this is true of each of us existing as one person in one nature, how much more true must it be of one person existing in two natures?

Much of the writing of Catholic theology in this area has focused on the question of Christ's immediate vision of God. It is striking that Catholic authors generally concede this in some form. Indeed Karl Rahner put it more strongly than that, declaring that there is a doctrine here which the theologian is not free to doubt.[1] It is in the interpretation of this vision that the authors diverge, but it can be taken as well established that, from the beginning of his time on earth, Jesus of Nazareth had an inner light, an effulgence of God, which guided his life in ways we cannot imagine. If we have difficulty in saying what this light was like, we can be bolder in saying a few things about what it was not. It may reasonably be maintained that it was not a kind of omniscience by which the child Jesus knew the answers to all our questions. It did not preclude a role for other processes of knowledge in virtue of which some meaning can be given to the notion of lack of knowledge in Christ. In particular, it did not mean that all through his life Jesus was haunted by the image of the cross.[2]

As a starting-point in approaching this mystery, it seems to this writer that something of Rahner's view of the place of Christ's vision of God in the entire scheme of things should be preserved. From the same author the distinction between reflexive and basic consciousness is also something to be retained. As we have seen, this principle has influenced both Balthasar and Lonergan, and indeed many others. It helps to explain how there can be real scope for progress in Christ's acquired knowledge and for the reality of human experience in his mental development. Problematic, however, is the way Rahner and Balthasar locate Christ's immediate vision of God within the pre-conceptual self-awareness of consciousness, taking the latter term in its strict sense. Here it seems to this writer that the approach of Lonergan and Crowe is much better grounded and yields better results. Rahner at least was more logical than Balthasar when he presented the immediate vision as Jesus' human soul knowing the Word, though this raised the spectre of a Nestorian duality of subjects. Lonergan's insistence on Christ's vision of God as knowledge rather than consciousness locates that vision within a relationship to an object of knowledge distinct from the knowing subject; and that fits the New Testament evidence for his continuous orientation to the Father.

Jesus' relationship to his Father is also the context within which a certain meaning can be given to the faith which moved our Lord in his life of surrender to a mysterious providence. Though this writer acknowledges this possibility, and the example of the three theologians studied in Chapter 7 points in the same direction, it seems to me, nevertheless, that the balance of the various factors favours a certain reticence about this form of language. In any acceptable interpretation the notion of faith is applied to our Lord only analogously, and it can easily obscure the uniqueness of Christ as knower and revealer. Lonergan made an apt comment when he remarked: 'Where all are believers and no one is a knower, no one's faith is reasonable.'[3] For these reasons it seems preferable that the predominant usage of the New Testament in avoiding the language of belief in the case of Christ should set the standard for our usage also; but I do not think that this precludes one building into one's final account Rahner's moving description of Jesus' ultimate surrender to the incomprehensibility of God.

The problem of lack of knowledge in Christ deserves a final statement. We have seen that Rahner, Balthasar and Lonergan, each in different ways, concede some meaning to this notion. Few issues so put to the test one's conception of the hypostatic union as this one does. Theologians commonly make a fundamental distinction which Lonergan formulates as one between nescience and ignorance. Nescience is the broader concept and refers to absence of knowledge generally, whereas ignorance indicates the lack of *due* knowledge, namely knowledge that one might be expected to have, given one's circumstances. An example of nescience is found in the way Jesus' human mind, even with the beatific vision, cannot encompass why God chose this order of providence. An example of ignorance would lie in the suggestion that Jesus did not know whether the Last Day would come soon or after centuries. Clearly the problem area lies in the latter case.

Another relevant distinction is that already referred to in the work of Rahner, namely that in all of us there are levels of knowing such that we can know something on one level and not know it on another. A young girl, for instance, might understand perfectly the concept of motherhood, but after she has actually become a mother she will understand it in a way she can scarcely have suspected before. The way we experience such levels of knowing is, of course, only an analogy for what theology would attribute to Christ, but it helps at least to remove the apparent contradiction which the hypothesis of different kinds of knowledge in Christ seems at first to establish. Rahner applied this principle especially to our Lord's awareness of his own divinity. Lonergan's approach allows it to be extended to the secondary objects of the beatific vision. Balthasar insisted that whatever special knowledge was to be attributed to Jesus was to be related always to his mission.[4]

This distinction is enhanced by that already made

between non-thematic and thematic knowledge. Something can be known on one level in a way one cannot put into words, while on the level of ordinary knowledge and communication it remains as yet unknown. It is necessary to keep both of these distinctions in mind when we close in for a final assessment of knowledge and ignorance in Christ. Hence it must be observed that the problem is broader than simply the question of beatific vision and infused knowledge. Even when the traditional triad in Christ's human knowledge is conceded, theologians have too easily tended to define the problem of Christ's knowledge in terms of these three levels of knowing. The hub of the difficulty, however, lies in how human knowing, even in the exceptional sense just referred to, can be combined with the reality of divine personhood and divine knowing. For the medievals there were ultimately *four* levels of knowing in Christ. Our Lord's special forms of human knowing become intelligible only as the counterpart within his humanity of something already present in some way within the divine personhood. The inescapable issue in all theories which propose a limitation in Christ's human knowing was that raised long ago by Gregory the Great: Unless you are a Nestorian, you cannot be an Agnoete.[5]

Whenever theologians and exegetes speak of Christ's knowing or not knowing this or that, it is always salutary to pose the question, Who is the 'he' to whom this knowledge or lack of it is being ascribed? Clearly a divine person knows all things, and wherever there is a divine person, divine knowledge has to be present, since personhood and knowledge are not really distinct in God. Now if there is only one person in Christ, and that person is divine, then divine knowledge is somehow present in the 'he' who carries out the various activities of Jesus of Nazareth. Clearly that is saying a great deal, and the problems of conceding to Christ special forms of *human* knowing pale into insignificance under the light of this divine presence.

Indeed this truth about divine personhood is so overwhelming that there is a tendency, whether consciously or unconsciously, to bracket it and to go on to discuss the problems of the three levels of Christ's human knowledge in isolation from it; but to do that is surely to divide Christ into two subjects: the divine 'he' who knows all things and is effectively, even if supposedly only provisionally, to be left out of account; and then this all too human 'he' who is simply so ignorant of so many things. This is precisely the option which many theologians have tried to avoid, though they differ so much in how they explain it. Rahner held that a purely ontic hypostatic union was impossible, namely one in being and not in consciousness.[6] If our explanation of Christ's lack of knowledge is driving us to posit a human 'he' independent of the divine person, then we seem to have crossed the line laid down by Gregory the Great between the orthodox on the one side and the Nestorian Agnoete on the other.

But there is another way, the one we have been trying to travel in this book. It is true that it does not yield a clear and distinct idea of how the various levels of knowing in Christ come together into one. Indeed, if we claimed to have such an idea, we would certainly be deluding ourselves. If the interiority of every human being is always mysterious even to close acquaintances, how much more so that of a person at once human and divine? But the inner mystery of the mind and heart of Christ is not totally opaque. From analogies in our own inner experience we can get glimpses from time to time that this mystery is not a contradiction. The ambivalent impression that emerges from the New Testament is confirmed by the complex deductions which Christian teachers and saints have been making over the centuries from the dogmatic-theological tradition.

Always theologians of Christology have to pick their steps between the docetic on the one hand and the Ebionite or adoptionist on the other. When the author of the Letter to the Hebrews wrote that Jesus was like us in all things but sin, he was scarcely attempting to sum up the whole of Christology in a phrase. Indeed if this phrase were driven to its literal ultimate, then Christ would be a human being and nothing more, even though sinless; but such a person could not be our redeemer. After all, we have such a sinless human being in Jesus' mother, but no serious theologian would claim that she could have redeemed the world.

At this point of our reflections it will be helpful to bring to mind that in the classical theology and spirituality of the

Church the question of Christ's knowledge was never separated from its larger context in redemption and grace. Perhaps under the influence of positivism and empiricism, we easily tend today to see the question as one simply of particular texts of scripture. For the ancients and medievals it was much more a question of the dogmatic-theological context. We will never understand, for instance, what people like Aquinas have in mind with their subtle and transcendent doctrine of Christ's knowledge, unless we see it, as they did, as part of the whole economy of salvation by which Christ is the perfect cause through which humanity will be brought to its perfection.

In the understanding of redemption today there is a fundamental divergence between those who see its purpose as simply humanization, and those who see it as that and something more, namely as divinization.[7] If redemption is seen to be adequately defined as the humanization of the world, there will be an inevitable tendency to reduce the image of the Saviour to his purely human activities. In this view, exemplarity will be the nub of his redemptive power. But if with the classical tradition one insists that the Saviour came to share our humanity that we might share in his divinity, then at the heart of the redemptive process efficient causality will be understood to be at work. We are saved not simply by Christ being what we are. He has to be more than we are if we are to be made other than we were. This needs to be spelt out a little more.

To the casual observer Christ's death on the cross was just another chapter in the history of man's inhumanity to man. To the one who sees Christ as simply the perfect human being sent by God, then his death will be appreciated as the supreme example of the gospel teaching on love and service. It will move us humanly on a psychological level by what can be called a moral or exemplary causality. But when Christ's paschal mystery is seen as that of the Son of God, then it will be believed to move us, not only humanly by the poignancy of its heroism, but in an even deeper way, on an ontological level, by the power of his divinity. It will be understood to remake us in his image, so that we are not only called but are sons and daughters of God.

The Christ who has come to transform us, does so, not

simply by being what we are, but by being more than we are. If Christ is human and nothing more, then, in the last analysis, his death can change nothing. At best it can only add the most moving chapter to the story of man's inhumanity to man. This might have a certain moral impact on subsequent generations, but it does not change the human situation fundamentally. Such a view scarcely does justice to the way Christian tradition has seen the death of Christ as the turning of the tide in the whole history of humanity's relationship with God. For the classical tradition, the opened side of Christ on the cross was the watershed of a new creation.

It is only within this context that we can appreciate the question of Christ's knowledge and consciousness. If Jesus is simply 'the man for others', 'saving' us by the moral power of his heroism, then indeed one need not expect him to be anything more than Schleiermacher described him – the highest instance of God-consciousness in our history. But if his very being among us is only conceived within a divine project for the transformation of the entire race through a personalized religion for each one, then it becomes more reasonable for us to find him carrying out his world-wide task, not as a dreamer not knowing what he was doing, but as a conscious and knowing person, with a unique perception of his task's scope and depth. He carried us all within him, said St Cyprian,[8] and, as the International Theological Commission realized in 1985, we cannot ignore the long tradition of spirituality which has taken Paul's words as applicable to each of us: 'He loved me and gave himself for me' (Gal 2:20).

The last quotation brings into focus the point where the problems of Christ's knowledge and consciousness are at their most acute, namely during his passion. Karl Rahner's suggestion of speaking rather of 'immediate vision' than of 'beatific vision' has been widely followed and, as we have seen, receives corroboration from the view of Aquinas that the vision of God in Christ's case could have been subject to a special providence by which the reality of his sufferings cannot be called into question.[9]

Our approach to the sufferings of Christ in Gethsemane and on the cross is given another dimension by recalling a major concern of contemporary soteriology ever since Auschwitz: does God suffer? Does the traditional doctrine of divine transcendence imply that God is simply above and beyond all suffering, serene in divine impassibility? In different ways, some acceptable, some not so, many theologians have come to admit that, just as the doctrine of the oneness and simplicity of God has to be qualified by the doctrine of the three persons, so that of his impassibility and immutability has to be qualified by the incarnation. God does not change in his divine nature, but he changes in something else, namely in Christ's humanity. Similarly, in Christ on the cross, God suffers. Part of the meaning of a divine person becoming human is precisely so that God can manifest in his Son how he suffers with us.

But there is more. In the passion of Christ God has become vulnerable. We know from Matthew 25:31ff how all the evil wrought by human beings on each other is ultimately done to Christ and through him to God. On the cross, Christ lets all that evil in some sense focus on himself. As well as being a crime against our fellow human beings, such evil is also a sin against God. On the cross, by being in the place of God and by being God, our Lord manifests before the world something of what sin is. In him we can see expressed, within the limits of a human life, the meaning of the horror of our history of sin as a rebellion against God and a rejection of his goodness. Such a load is quasi-infinite in its scope and in its depth, and so the human experience of Christ can only be an expression within the limits of the finite of what the anguish of such a quasi-infinite burden might be. No wonder that the weight of it drove the blood through his pores and wrung from him such cries as we hear about in the New Testament (Mark 15:34; Heb 5:7).

What the inner meaning of such anguish might be is of course beyond us, but there are two points I would wish to maintain as against common assumptions. Many commentators have been content to take the cry of the psalmist on the lips of Christ in Mark 15:34 as both historically and literally true in the sense of an abandonment of the Son by the Father. For my part, this seems to me to be going too far. The depth and mysteriousness of the suffering to which the evangelist here refers is certainly beyond our imagining, but to press the quotation to the point that one implies that the union between Christ and his Father was ever broken seems unsustainable in the case of a divine person.[10] Even though the face of God was seen by our Lord only as through a dark ravine of suffering, there must always have been, if Jesus is truly united with God, some light at the end of that darkness. According to Rahner, when Christ on the cross said 'Father', his surrender was illuminated by 'a final secret light'.[11] One exegete put it paradoxically: 'The "Why" left without an answer (Mark 15:34) is the affirmation of the supreme and indestructible bond which unites the Son with his Father.'[12]

The second point I wish to make confronts those who would see a contradiction between the reality of Christ's sufferings and the notion of his immediate vision of God. It seems to me that one can argue that, far from mitigating his sufferings, our Lord's union with the Father in knowledge must have increased them all the more. The more sensitive people are, the more they are capable of suffering. No human being has ever been as sensitive to the goodness of God as was our Lord with his unique knowledge and vision of the Father. This would have given him an insight into the horror of sin and the enormity of blasphemy as it weighed upon him in that mysterious experience where his sufferings were not only vicarious for his fellow human beings but, in another sense, vicarious for his Father in heaven.

It has been suggested that we might have some remote parallel for this trial of Jesus in the dark night of the spirit as our great mystics have experienced it. We often notice in the lives of the saints a strange paradox: the deeper their appreciation of the things of God, the greater the darkness they have to endure. As they enter into realms of that union so far beyond the imagination of ordinary believers, the saints can find themselves at times in regions of anguish which also pass our comprehension. Physically our Lord's sufferings were not the most extreme in the history of human torture. Only if one takes account of his unique inner spirit can one be open to a statement such as that of Balthasar: 'His unique hypostatic suffering embraces every temporal and eternal suffering possible to a created human being.'[13] At the same time we might bear in mind another aspect of the paradoxes of mysticism: even the very bitterness can have its sweetness, and even the very darkness can dazzle.

In those black moments of life, when we believers find

ourselves struggling with the burden of our mortality through some dark night of faith, we inevitably wish to draw strength by attributing to Jesus the same kind of struggle and the same kind of darkness as we are undergoing; but in fact, if the truth were told, it is more likely that our Lord only experienced the counterpart of our anguish by its being elevated to a unique degree of intensity, commensurate with the uniqueness of his being, as he, the absolute Saviour, entered into the ultimate struggle of good with evil. It is impossible for us to conceive what such a confrontation might have been like, but the language of the New Testament seems to suggest that it consisted less in simple blind endurance than in some achievement in which knowledge and discernment played a part; indeed it seems to point to the ultimate vanquishing of darkness by light, and to the unmasking of the forces of evil and deceit, which lie hidden at the heart of the world.[14]

The final aspect of the passion that remains to be clarified is that brought before us by the quotation from Galatians 2:20. Did Christ in his passion know me and love me? It is the same point as that raised towards the end of the statement of the International Theological Commission in 1985. There the answer lay in having recourse to Christ's divine knowledge, and this may well be the most one can say, though it scarcely fits in with Paul's usual way of speaking of Christ. This is where the whole question of the secondary objects of the beatific vision becomes relevant. In line with that tradition there is the passage of Pius XI in his encyclical, *Miserentissimus Redemptor*, where he explicitly envisages the sins of each of us as coming before the mind of Christ in Gethsemane. This is really to rely on a 'mirror image' concept of the beatific vision from which much of contemporary theology has distanced itself. Other theologians will go to the other extreme and exclude any such objects from their notion of the vision, but the problem with that is that it hardly does justice to the tradition of spirituality and to the immediacy with which people, from Ignatius of Antioch to Julian of Norwich, have meditated on the passion over the centuries.

A middle position is that of Bernard Lonergan. While rejecting the 'mirror image' approach to the vision of God, he is still open to giving the secondary objects some reality within the human mind of Christ as part of that non-thematic and global grasp of things which for him is an aspect of the vision of God. In this way he can give more reality to the statement of Paul than is allowed for in the account of the Theological Commission, but what this would mean in the actual thematic knowledge of Christ in his passion is something that, absolutely speaking, we do not know. We could, however, hazard the opinion that, on his way to his death, the thematic awareness of Christ was scarcely focused on these aspects but on the mystery of anguish which was laying siege to every outer and inner sense that he had.

Karl Rahner once remarked that theologians can sometimes be too knowledgeable; our topic seems to be one of the cases where Rahner's caution is particularly relevant. Apophatic spirituality has made us more aware that 'the soul approaches God more nearly by not understanding than by understanding'.[15] Surely there must be something corresponding in theology when it comes to speak of a divine person. There must be a sense in which our Christology has to be apophatic also, when eventually we acknowledge that, in the last analysis, we do not know how divine and human come together in Christ. This limitation on our understanding extends both to his being and to his knowledge. Jesus remains as mysterious for us as he did for the author of the Messianic Secret in Mark's Gospel. The most we can do is to remove the apparent contradictions and to set down a few parameters within which we consider that the answer ultimately lies, but it is an answer that in this life remains unattainable in its details.

At the same time the results of our enquiry are not totally negative. At the end of his book on this subject Riedlinger attempted to sum up his idea of Christ's knowledge in a phrase which might be translated as 'immediacy to God in history'.[16] It is a good phrase, since it brings together two sides of a paradox. On the one hand there has to be in the Word made flesh an immediacy to God by which he knows the Father in a manner beyond our imagining. By this we exclude the image of a self-doubting rabbi not knowing who he is or what he is doing. On the other hand we acknowledge that this immediacy to God does not remove the incarnate Word from the course of human history. By this we rule out the notion of a timeless omniscient being engaged in a pedagogy of pretence. To throw some light on how these two aspects might come together into one is precisely the theological task we have been endeavouring to explore. However, at the end of the day, the only complete certainty lies in affirming the truth in both sides of the paradox and in acknowledging the mystery.

NOTES

1  TI 5 (1966), p. 215.
2  On the influence of such an idea on spirituality, see J. de Guibert, *Leçons de théologie spirituelle* (Toulouse: Editions de la Revue d'Ascétique et de Mystique, 1955), p. 206.
3  Lonergan, *De Verbo incarnato*, p. 391.
4  Balthasar, *Theodrama*, p. 173. Torrell considers that Aquinas' view of infused knowledge had the same focus, 'S. Thomas d'Aquin', p. 406, citing ST, III, q. 15, a. 4.
5  DS 476.
6  TI 5 (1966), p. 206.
7  This divergence is pointed out in the second of the four official texts on Christology discussed in the preceding chapter. See Sharkey (ed.), *International Theological Commission*, pp. 212f, where the term used is 'hominization'.
8  Cyprian, *Letter* 63 (PL 4:383; RJ 583).
9  See Chapter 5 above, references at n. 20.
10  Some writers point out that the perspective of Mark 15:34 must have included Psalm 21(22) in its entirety, and so the words of consolation at the end of the psalm, e.g. Schillebeeckx, *Christ*, p. 824. This opinion, however, enjoys no consensus.
11  K. Rahner, *The Love of Jesus and the Love of Neighbour*, p. 45.
12  Guillet, *La foi de Jésus-Christ*, p. 93. See the whole section in Guillet, *ibid.*, pp. 88–94.
13  Balthasar, *New Elucidations* (San Francisco: Ignatius Press, 1986), p. 116.
14  Cf. John 1:5; 3:20–21; Ephes 6:10–13.
15  John of the Cross, 'Living Flame of Love', stanza III, no. 48, *The Complete Works of Saint John of the Cross* (London: Burns, Oates & Washbourne, 1953), vol. III, p. 168.
16  In German the phrase is 'geschichtliche Gottesschau', Riedlinger, *Geschichtlichkeit und Vollendung*, pp. 158–60. Riedlinger, however, interprets the phrase in a manner closer to that of Rahner, where my approach is closer to that of Lonergan.

# ⊠ Bibliography

H. U. von Balthasar, 'La conscience de Jésus et sa mission', *Communio* 4, no. 1 (1979) pp. 31–40.

H. U. von Balthasar, *Does Jesus Know Me? Do We Know Him?* (San Francisco: Ignatius Press, 1983).

H. U. von Balthasar, *New Elucidations* (San Francisco: Ignatius Press, 1986).

H. U. von Balthasar, *La foi du Christ* (Paris: Aubier, 1968).

H. U. von Balthasar, *The Glory of the Lord: A Theological Aesthetics*, seven volumes (Edinburgh: T. & T. Clark, 1982–89).

H. U. von Balthasar, *Spouse of the Word* (Explorations in Theology II; San Francisco: Ignatius Press, 1991).

H. U. von Balthasar, *Theodrama: Theological Dramatic Theory* III: *Dramatis Personae: The Person in Christ* (San Francisco: Ignatius, 1992).

H. U. von Balthasar, *A Theology of History* (London: Sheed & Ward, 1964).

Bonaventure, *Opera omnia*, tome 4: *In tertium librum sententiarum* (Paris: Vivès, 1865).

R. Brown, *The Gospel according to John: I–XII* (New York: Doubleday, 1982).

R. Brown, *An Introduction to New Testament Christology* (London: Chapman, 1994).

R. Brown, *Jesus God and Man: Modern Biblical Reflections* (London: Chapman, 1968).

F. Crowe, 'Eschaton and worldly mission in the mind and heart of Jesus' in *The Eschaton: A Community of Love*, ed. J. Papin (Vilanova, PA: Vilanova University Press 1971), pp. 105–44.

O. Cullmann, *The Christology of the New Testament* (London: SCM Press, 1959).

B. de Margerie, *The Human Knowledge of Christ* (Boston: St Paul, 1980).

F. Dreyfus, *Jésus savait-il qu'il était Dieu?* (Paris: Cerf, 1984).

J. D. Dunn, *Jesus and the Spirit: A Study of the Religious and Charismatic Experience of Jesus and the First Christians as Reflected in the New Testament* (The New Testament Library, no. 9; London: SCM Press, 1975).

J. Duns Scotus, *Opera omnia*, tome 14: *Quaestiones in tertium librum Sententiarum (Opus oxoniense)* (Paris: Vivès, 1894).

C. Duquoc, *Christologie: Essai dogmatique*, tome 1: *L'homme Jésus*; tome 2: *Le Messie* (Collection 'Cogitatio fidei' nos. 29 and 67; Paris: Cerf, 1968 and 1974).

J. T. Ernst, *Die Lehre der hochmittelalterlichen Theologen von der volkommenen Erkenntnis Christi: Ein Versuch zur Auslegung der klassischen Dreiteilung: Visio Beata, Scientia Infusa und Scientia Acquisita* (Freiburg–Basle–Vienna: Herder, 1971).

J. A. Fitzmyer (ed.), *Scripture and Christology: A Statement of the Biblical Commission with a Commentary* (London: Chapman, 1986).

R. H. Fuller, *The Foundations of New Testament Christology* (New York: Scribners, 1965).

J. Galot, *La coscienza di Gesù* (Assisi: Cittadella, 1974).

J. Galot, 'Le Christ terrestre et la vision', *Gregorianum* 67 (1986), pp. 429–50.

J. Galot, *Who is Christ? A Theology of the Incarnation* (Rome: Gregorian University Press, 1980).

A. Gore, *Dissertations on Subjects Connected with the Incarnation* (London: John Murray, 1907).

A. Grillmeier and H. Bacht (eds.), *Das Konzil von Chalkedon: Geschichte und Gegenwart*, Band III: *Chalkedon heute* (Würzburg: Echterverlag, 1954).

A. Grillmeier, *Christ in Christian Tradition*, vol. I: *From the Apostolic Age to Chalcedon (AD 451)* (London: Mowbray, 1975); vol. II: *From the Council of Chalcedon (451) to Gregory the Great (590–604)*, Part 2: *The Church of Constantinople in the Sixth Century*, with Theresia Hainthaler (London: Mowbray, 1995).

J. Guillet, *La foi de Jésus-Christ* (Collection 'Jésus et Jésus-Christ' no. 12; Paris: Desclée, 1980).

E. Gutwenger, 'The Problem of Christ's Knowledge', *Concilium* 2 (January 1966), pp. 48–55.

L. Iammarone, 'La visione beatifica di Cristo viatore nel pensiero di San Tommaso', *Doctor Communis* 36 (1983), pp. 287–330.

*International Theological Commission: Texts and Documents 1969–1985*, ed. M. Sharkey (San Francisco: Ignatius, 1989).

J. Jeremias, *New Testament Theology*, vol. 1: *The Proclamation of Jesus* (New Testament Library, no. 12; London: SCM Press, 1971).

C. Kannengiesser, *Athanase d'Alexandrie, évêque et écrivain: une lecture des traités 'Contre les Ariens'* (Collection 'Théologie historique' no. 70) (Paris: Beauchesne, 1983).

W. Kasper, *Jesus the Christ* (London: Burns & Oates, 1976).

J. Lebreton, *History of the Dogma of the Trinity: From Its Origins to the Council of Nicaea*, vol. I: *The Origins* (London: Burns Oates & Washbourne, 1939).

J. Liebaert, *La doctrine christologique de saint Cyrille d'Alexandrie avant la querelle nestorienne* (Lille: Faculté Catholique, 1951).

B. Lonergan, 'Christology today: methodological reflections' in *A Third Collection: Papers by Bernard J. F. Lonergan, S.J.*, ed. F. E. Crowe (New York: Paulist/London: Chapman, 1985), pp. 74–99.

B. Lonergan, *De constitutione Christi ontologica et psychologica* (Rome:

Gregorian University Press, 1961).

B. Lonergan, *A Second Collection: Papers by Bernard Lonergan*, ed. W. F. Ryan and B. J. Tyrrell (London: Darton, Longman & Todd, 1974).

B. Lonergan, *A Third Collection: Papers by Bernard Lonergan* (New York: Paulist/London: Chapman, 1985).

B. Lonergan, *De Verbo incarnato*, ad usum auditorum editio tertia (Rome: Gregorian University, 1964).

J. Macquarrie, *Jesus Christ in Modern Thought* (London: SCM Press/Philadelphia: Trinity Press International, 1990).

J. Maritain, *On the Grace and Humanity of Jesus* (London: Burns & Oates, 1969).

E. L. Mascall, *Christ, the Christian and the Church: A Study of the Incarnation and its Consequences* (London: Longmans Green & Co., 1946).

J. A. McGuckin, *St. Cyril of Alexandria: The Christological Controversy, Its History, Theology and Texts* (Leiden: Brill, 1994).

J. P. Meier, *A Marginal Jew: Rethinking the Historical Jesus*, vol. 1: *The Roots of the Problem and the Person* (New York/London: Doubleday, 1991); vol. 2: *Mentor, Message and Miracles* (New York/London: Doubleday, 1994).

R. Moloney, 'Approaches to Christ's knowledge in the patristic era' in *Studies in Patristic Christology: Proceedings of the Third Maynooth Patristic Conference*, ed. T. Finan and V. Twomey (Dublin: Four Courts Press, 1998), pp. 37–66.

R. Moloney, 'The mind of Christ in transcendental theology: Rahner, Lonergan, Crowe', *Heythrop Journal* 25 (1984), pp. 288–300.

R. Moloney, 'Patristic approaches to Christ's knowledge', *Milltown Studies* no. 37 (Spring 1996), pp. 65–81; no. 38 (Autumn 1996), pp. 34–47.

W. G. Most, *The Consciousness of Christ* (Front Royal, Virginia: Christendom Publications, 1980).

C. F. D. Moule, *The Phenomenon of the New Testament* (Collection 'Studies in Biblical Theology' Second Series no. 1; London: SCM Press, 1967).

J. Neuner and J. Dupuis (eds.), *The Christian Faith in the Doctrinal Documents of the Catholic Church* (London: Collins, 1986).

*The New Jerome Biblical Commentary*, ed. by R. Brown, J. Fitzmyer and R. Murphy (London: Chapman, 1990).

J. H. Newman, *Select Treatises of S. Athanasius of Alexandria in Controversy with the Arians* (Oxford: J. H. Parker, 1844).

M.-J. Nicholas, 'Voir Dieu dans la "condition charnelle"', *Doctor Communis* 36 (1983), pp. 384–94.

F. Ocáriz, L. F. Mateo Seco and J. A. Riestra, *The Mystery of Jesus Christ: A Christology and Soteriology Textbook* (Dublin: Four Courts Press, 1994).

G. O'Collins, *Christology: A Biblical, Historical and Systematic Study of Jesus* (Oxford: Oxford University Press, 1995).

D. Ols, *Le cristologie contemporanee e le loro posizioni fondamentali al vaglio della dottrina di S. Tommaso* (Collection 'Studi Tomistici' no. 39; Rome: Pontificiale Accademia di S. Tommaso, 1991).

J. C. O'Neill, *Who Did Jesus Think He Was?* (Leiden: Brill, 1995).

W. Pannenberg, *Jesus God and Man* (London: SCM Press, 1976).

N. Pittenger, *Catholic Faith in a Process Perspective* (New York: Orbis, 1981).

N. Pittenger, *Christology Reconsidered* (London : SCM Press, 1970).

N. Pittenger, *Christ and Christian Faith* (New York: Round Table Press, 1941).

N. Pittenger, *Process Thought and Christian Faith* (New York: Macmillan, 1968).

N. Pittenger, *The Word Incarnate* (London: James Nisbet, 1959).

K. Rahner, 'Current problems in Christology', *Theological Investigations*, vol. 1 (London: Darton, Longman & Todd, 1961), pp. 168–74.

K. Rahner, 'Dogmatic reflections on the knowledge and self-consciousness of Christ', *Theological Investigations*, vol. 5 (London: Darton, Longman & Todd, 1966), pp. 193–215.

K. Rahner, *Foundations of Christian Faith* (London: Darton, Longman & Todd, 1978).

K. Rahner, *The Love of Jesus and the Love of Neighbour* (Slough: St Paul, 1983).

K. Rahner, 'Two basic types of Christology', *Theological Investigations*, vol. 13 (London: Darton, Longman & Todd, 1975), pp. 213–23.

H. Riedlinger, *Geschichtlichkeit und Vollendung des Wissens Christi* (Collection 'Quaestiones Disputatae' no. 32; Freiburg–Basle–Vienna: Herder, 1966).

J. M. Salgado, 'La science du Fils de Dieu fait homme. Prises de position des Pères et du pré-scolastique. IIe -XIIe siècle', *Doctor Communis* 36 (1983), pp. 180–286.

E. Schillebeeckx, *Jesus: An Experiment in Christology* (London: Collins, 1979).

F. Schleiermacher, *The Christian Faith* (Edinburgh: T. & T. Clark, 1960).

P. Schoonenberg, *The Christ* (London/Sydney: Sheed & Ward, 1972).

P. Schoonenberg, 'Het avontuur der christologie', *Tijdschrift voor Theologie* 12 (1972), pp. 307–32.

P. Schoonenberg, 'Process or History in God?' *Louvain Studies* 4 (1973), pp. 303–19, summarized in *Theology Digest* 23 (1975), pp. 38–44.

H. Schürmann, *Comment Jésus a-t-il vécu sa mort?* (Collection 'Lectio Divina' no. 93; Paris: Cerf, 1977).

B. Sesboüé, *Jésus-Christ dans la tradition de l'église* (Collection 'Jésus et Jésus-Christ' no. 12; Paris: Desclée, 1982).

B. Sesboüé, *Pédagogie du Christ: Eléments de christologie fondamentale* (Paris: Cerf, 1995).

J. Ternus, 'Das Seelen- und Bewusstseinsleben Jesu: Problemge-schichtlich-systematische Untersuchung' in *Das Konzil von Chalkedon: Geschichte und Gegenwart*, ed. A. Grillmeier and H. Bacht (Würzburg: Echterverlag 1954), vol. III, pp. 81–237.

J. P. Torrell, 'S. Thomas d'Aquin et la science du Christ: Une relecture des questions 9–12 de la "Tertia pars" de la Somme de Théologie' in *Saint Thomas au XXe siècle: Actes du colloque du centenaire de la "Revue Thomiste" 25–28 mars 1993 – Toulouse*, ed. Serge-Thomas Bonino (Paris:

Editions Saint Paul, 1994), pp. 394–409.

T. J. van Bavel, *Recherches sur la christologie de saint Augustin: l'humain et le divin dans le Christ d'après saint Augustin* (Fribourg: Editions Universitaires, 1954).

G. Vass, *A Pattern of Christian Doctrines*, part 1: *God and Christ* (Understanding Karl Rahner, vol. 3; London: Sheed & Ward, 1996).

A. Voegtle, 'Exegetische Erwägungen über das Wissen und Selbstbewusstsein Jesu' in *Gott in Welt: Festgabe für Karl Rahner*, ed. H. Vorgrimler (Freiburg: Herder, 1964), vol. I, pp. 608–67.

E.-H. Wéber, *Dialogue et dissensions entre saint Bonaventure et saint Thomas d'Aquin à Paris (1252–1273)* (Collection 'Bibliothèque Thomiste' no. 41; Paris: Librairie Philosophique J. Vrin, 1974).

E.-H. Wéber, *Le Christ selon Saint Thomas d'Aquin* (Collection 'Jésus et Jésus-Christ' dirigée par Joseph Doré, no. 35; Paris: Desclée, 1988).

## ▨ Index

Printed in Great Britain by
Amazon.co.uk, Ltd.,
Marston Gate.

⊠ *The Knowledge of Christ*

# ⊠ PROBLEMS IN THEOLOGY

In the study of Christian theology, there have been, over the centuries, a number of problems for which no adequate explanation has yet been given, or at least, none given which commands substantial agreement among those whose task it is to explain the faith. Some of these issues are central to the understanding of Christianity – the nature of Christ's presence in the Eucharist, for example, or the need for, and the achievement of, redemption. Books in this series will look at crucial topics of this kind. Written by experts, each volume will both trace the history of attempts to answer a particular problem in theology, and then propose a new understanding of the doctrine under debate. Though based upon the latest scholarship, the books are intended for the serious enquirer as much as for the professional theologian.

*Already published:*

*The Atonement*
MICHAEL WINTER

*The Eucharist*
RAYMOND MOLONEY SJ

*The Knowledge of Christ*
RAYMOND MOLONEY SJ